THE CLAIM GAME

THE CLAIM GAME

Twenty Best Practices When Managing and Investigating Workers' Comp Claims

Mario S. Pecoraro

CEO of Alliance Worldwide Investigative Group

THE CLAIM GAME
Twenty Best Practices When Managing and Investigating Workers' Comp Claims

iUniverse books may be ordered through booksellers or by contacting:

iUniverse
1663 Liberty Drive
Bloomington, IN 47403
www.iuniverse.com
1-800-Authors (1-800-288-4677)

ISBN: 978-1-4917-7414-4 (sc)
ISBN: 978-1-4917-7415-1 (e)

Library of Congress Control Number: 2015914729

Print information available on the last page.

iUniverse rev. date: 10/06/2015

TABLE OF CONTENTS

INTRODUCTION

How NOT to Get Your Butt Kicked in a Workers' Comp Claim

While most kids were playing ball and hanging out on street corners after school, I already had a part-time job: riding along with my Mom and Dad while they did investigations on behalf of their small, family-owned private investigation firm.

It was the only business I ever knew. It was what my parents talk about at breakfast, lunch and dinner, and I got hooked from a very young age. How young? I can remember being twelve or thirteen years old and riding along with my folks as they did surveillance, tracked down missing persons and pursued various leads.

I can even recall having to enter a shopping mall after a subject to try to find out what they were up to – who would have ever suspected a twelve-year- old investigating someone? Nobody! In retrospect, it was probably the perfect "cover" for doing surveillance.

As I got older, in my later teens and in high school, I became more involved in the family business, conducting hundreds and hundreds of hours in the field doing investigations. I participated in everything from locating witnesses and missing persons, to conducting interviews, to performing covert surveillance. I also performed undercover investigative operations, and later trained new investigators in techniques for the family business. I even met with clients and, eventually, handled my own investigations.

Even though I was barely old enough to drive at the time, I have fond memories of travelling to various courthouses at a ripe "old" age of seventeen. I conducted hundreds of background investigations on a regular basis, often times travelling more than 120-150 miles from home to complete investigations.

After high school I worked nonstop while pursuing my Bachelor of Science degree in Criminal Justice with a double major in Italian from the State University of New York at Albany, where I graduated Cum Laude. You may wonder why Italian? The answer is simple: it was the second language spoken growing up in my household and the result of a proud Italian heritage that I have come to enjoy so much.

Finally, it was time to put all that investigate experience to good use. In 2005 I founded Alliance Worldwide Investigative Group, which specializes in helping organizations of all sizes in managing risk from an investigative perspective at all levels; from pre-employment to post hire challenges. My work ranges from background screening to insurance and other fraud investigations.

Over time, Alliance has grown into a national/international investigative firm offering a variety of services. We focus on helping organizations increase their bottom line, and manage challenges that are associated with an organization's most critical assets: its people, often called "human capital".

With more than twenty years of proven experience in due-diligence based investigative services, Alliance

Worldwide Investigative Group has become a leader in the insurance and background investigation fields, property and casualty adjusting and process service industries.

Prior to founding the company, I worked for more than fifteen years as a private investigator in my parents' firm and conducted in excess of 2,500 hours of field investigative work, skip-tracing, and asset investigations, and located missing persons, heirs and witnesses.

In addition, I serve on the executive boards of many industry organizations and community not-for-profit organizations. I have been asked to participate in forums and give presentations on best practices in the industry, from my experiences.

I am often sought out as an expert on investigative matters and have been featured on local and national media outlets. I conduct lectures and speaking engagements throughout New York State and was recently honored by my peers as an "Outstanding Business Person."

In other words, investigation – in all its forms – is all I've ever known.

So that's me; now let's talk about you:

Human Resources, Workers' Comp and YOU

I'll assume that, if you're reading a book called **The Claim Game:** *20 Best Practices When Managing and Investigating Workers' Comp Claims*, you're somehow responsible for managing risk in your organization, and/or that you're either currently facing – or looking to avoid facing – staggering losses as a result of one or more workers' comp claims.

The good news is, you're not alone. Employers throughout the country are often faced with the difficult decisions of how to handle claims. And, whether they are handled internally through an in-house claims group or outsourced to a Third Party Administrator or Carrier, employers ultimately have full control over the entire process. Employers often times face serious workers' comp issues and steps may be taken prior to and throughout the course of employment to help mitigate these risks.

This book will be a key resource for employers throughout the country, but also serve as a tool that can be used to help them and their claims partners navigate the world of risk as it relates to Workers' Compensation Claims.

How? By giving you the tools you need to fight back against workers' comp before the first claim is ever filed. It all starts with Human Resources. Why? Because that's every company's clearinghouse for vital employee information.

Think about it: from interview to disciplinary action to award to recognition to insurance to termination, it all has to go through the employee's Human Resources file.

This book will teach you how to get into the habit of gathering data on every employee, from the first interview onward, in order to protect yourself against crippling workers' comp claims later on. If managed properly, employee files bursting with such information can be an asset to the investigation, and often save the company thousands, if not hundreds of thousands, of dollars.

Consider the following scenario to see how this might all play out: a potential employee comes in for an interview and answers the usual questions. In the course of the interview, he shares several tidbits of information that can be easily, and dutifully, noted by the interviewer. For instance:

- **He's in a bowling league**
- **He enjoys fishing and water sports as a hobby**
- **He runs a fishing blog and is active in social media**
- **He's married with two children**

While this may sound like so much background information designed to ensure that the applicant is a good fit with your company, it can also become vital information if he becomes an employee and eventually makes a workers' comp claim.

It can also be useful in preventing a claim by leading to an early dismissal. For instance, let's say you hire this employee, he does a good job for a few months or even a few years, and then things start to slip. He frequently calls in sick, sometimes with a medical excuse, sometimes without.

Since your HR person took great care to list all his extracurricular activities, Facebook page, website, blog, interests, etc., with a few routine searches it can be easy to find out that, let's say, he was at a softball tournament two towns over when he claimed he had the flu. Depending on your tolerance policy, that could be grounds for immediate dismissal, reprimand or a variety of options in between.

Either way, documenting such inconsistencies provides a wealth of information, background and benefits if the employee later makes a claim. It's also at the heart of the philosophy of this book, which is a simple one: the best offense is a good defense!

Parting Words

Regardless of the size of your company, or your position in it, this book can save you the time, energy, manpower and money that costs other companies tens of thousands of dollars in workers' comp claim payouts.

Here you'll discover:

- *Preventive Maintenance Through Human Resources*
- *Incident and Risk*
- *Investigations 101*
- *Examine the Nature of the Request*
- *Types of Investigation*
- *The Secrets of Surveillance*
- *How to Assess Your Provider*
- *And, best of all… How NOT to Get Your Butt Kicked in a Workers' Comp Claim*

And that's just the beginning! If you're ready, everything you ever wanted to know about how to protect yourself from workers' comp claims, but were afraid to ask, starts on the very next page.

CHAPTER 1

Your Best Defense is a Good Offense – What Employers Should Do **Before** a Hiring Decision is Made

Believe it or not, the best way of defending yourself from a lengthy, ugly and costly workers' comp claim happens well before a hiring decision is made.

Companies that are aware of the high cost of bad hiring decisions recognize the importance of having a pre-screening strategy in place, one that begins with the first point of contract for potential new hires.

This chapter will lay the groundwork for your own best defense against workers' comp claims by making you aware of both the high cost of bad hiring decisions, as well as the importance of putting in place a strong strategy of proactive HR principles from day one.

By the Numbers: *The High Cost of a Bad Hire*

We all know hiring a bad fit for a great position can be inconvenient, but it can also be extremely costly. In this section I'll run through the various specific costs of a bad hire, and let you feel their cumulative effect for yourself.

Resume Fraud: *The Ticking Time Bomb*

Employee fraud often begins before an interview, with the first document you see: their resume. In fact, a recent study on resume fraud concluded that, "Fifty-three percent of resumes and job applications contain falsifications," including fudged job titles, degrees, dates and salary.

That's why it's so critical to have background checks in place as standard hiring procedure. But don't just take my word for it. According to the Society for Human Resource Management, "Background verification services are essential…"

Business Failure

Can a business actually fail because of a bad hire – or even a few? You wouldn't necessarily consider business failure a likely result of employee fraud, but the government does. In fact, the US Department of Commerce claims that "One-third of all business failures are the result of employee theft or other employee crime."

Employee Theft

Employee theft is obviously another huge issue, and a direct cost to the company of a bad hire. Statistic Brain asserts that, "$50 billion is stolen annually in U.S. businesses by employees." This cost adds, cumulatively, to lost profits, productivity and morale.

Loss of Business

Imagine if your bad hire is a key employee, a member of the sales force, or the only one in the office who knows how to do inventory – or payroll.

The loss of business while replacing this bad hire – finding a replacement, training them and getting them up to speed, can cost thousands or millions, depending on the volatility of the market and size of your business.

Direct Costs to the Organization

It's hard to put a true price tag on the cost of a bad hire on an entire organization, because of course every organization is different. But we can apply a rough estimate based on a variety of credible sources.

For instance, the U.S. Department of Labor estimates that the cost of a bad hire to an organization can range from thirty percent of an individuals' first year income. And according to Tony Hsieh, CEO of Zappos, the cost can run as much as millions.

Employee Morale

One of the key costs of making a bad hiring decision is the ripple effect it has across several layers of an organization, from peers and coworkers, to managers, to the overall company. One of these key costs is employee morale.

Consider a bad hire misses deadlines, performs poorly, doesn't play well with others, arrives late, leaves early, and misses too many days. Now other workers – good, productive, valued workers – have to take up the slack. This is not fair to them, of course, but it also impacts employee morale, work productivity, safety, security, culture and more!

Most bad hires come with more than just the label of "bad hire." They tend to have bad attitudes that permeate the organization's culture, and eventually have a significant bad impact on the rest of the team!

Momentum

A hidden cost we often overlook is that of momentum. All companies thrive on it, and bad employees rob it from us. When they're on a team, they break our concentration, force us to slow down and let them catch up, or put a burden on other team members who must take up their slack. When they deal with customers, we often spend time making up for their mistakes, either by doing damage control, or offering refunds, coupons, passes or special perks.

Time

Consider time lost – and we all know time is money – in having to deal with a bad hire by all parties involved in the process. First there is the time wasted during the person's employ: in training them, often retraining them, cleaning up their mistakes, farming off duties they can't perform to others on the team, waiting for them to deliver, and dealing with their missed deadlines.

Then there is the additional time – and cost – of firing and replacing them: another job search, more lost time while the position isn't filled, training the "new" new hire, etc. Now, multiply that by the number of people who were involved in the entire process – and we're talking hundreds of hours and dollars are gone, wasted!

Overall Cost Over the Life of Employment

Finally, let's see why Zappos CEO Tony Hsieh says that bad hires can cost a company "millions" over the life of his or her employment. It may sound inflated, particularly if you run a small- to medium-size company. However, consider the following typical scenario and, after we walk through it together, perhaps we'll both see why that figure may not be too far off the mark after all.

Let's say you hire "John," a new employee at your real estate investment firm. John looks good on paper. You needed someone fast, so the hire made sense...at the time. So you spend a few weeks interviewing him, which takes time from your Human Resources department, hiring team, managers and team leaders.

Now that John's on board, you've got another forty-five to sixty days invested in training him in your routines, software, proprietary methods, customs and processes. That's time away from regular teamwork, team meetings, waiting for him to get up to speed, putting off deadlines, not to mention the training and preparation by many members of a team.

Meanwhile, the others in the organization are picking up the slack and over time it is learned that maybe it would have been best if John had never been hired in the first place. Now there you are: everyone's job is harder because of one bad hire, and you still have to fire John, start the search for his replacement all over again, and hire and train another new hire for the next forty-five to sixty days of lost, or at least reduced, momentum.

What time and energy has been invested by all parties? How much time was invested by human resources, team members, team leaders, managers and department heads? And what is all this time, energy and manpower worth?

And don't forget: this doesn't even begin to mention the potential background breach presented by introducing John to all your proprietary information during his employ, or the potential harm caused should John have a fraud or workers' comp issue once employed. What if he takes your client lists, leads or other potentially valuable information to his next job? How much might those lost sales cost down the road? What kind of negative impact, beyond the hiring, training, firing and manpower costs, could this one bad hire of "John" have on the organization as a whole?

Perhaps now that million dollar cost might not seem so far off the mark!

Never Compromise on Culture and Integrity: *Best Practices for Making the Best Hire*

So, how do we avoid mishaps like "John" and all the other bad hires lurking out there? How do we avoid the costs of hiring, training and ultimately firing a "bad fit," as well as avoid the costly issue of a bad hire turning our loss into their gain by fraudulently filing a workers comp claim?

In my opinion, and decades of experience, the best defense against employee misdeeds, theft and fraud is always a good offense. By now you have seen firsthand the staggering costs of a single hiring misfire, let alone the repeat of continual bad hires all year, every year.

Putting a strategic game plan in place for every new hire, every time, every day, week, month and year is going to reduce costs on the back end and, save your company – potentially – millions of dollars in the long run.

The following are some specific points on how to craft your own hiring plan.

Culture Clash and Core Values

You have to hire for culture and core values, *period*. Workforces are made up of teams, even if they're very small ones, and if the new hire doesn't fit the culture, or the core values you and the rest of your people hold dear, you're never going to "force" that kind of fit no matter how good he or she looks on paper. You should know what your organization's core values are and be ready to hire and fire by them!

One way to test for culture is to, once you've narrowed down a candidate or two, "test float" a potential team situation by having the team take the candidate to lunch, or a movie or some other "field" trip where they can be observing for any "red flags" that might indicate this isn't a great fit. As we've just seen, the price of an afternoon off for a few employees is far outweighed by the costs of making a bad hire.

Assessment Testing

Job assessments are critical for ensuring that a new hire is not only a good fit for the team, but also up to the job requirements themselves. For instance:

- Is there a skills match?
- Are they up to the job, physically speaking?
- Is the work feasible for the skills they possess?

Application

Much like a resume, a prospect's job application can often be the first sign of trouble that you're headed for a bad hire. While most prospective employees endeavor to be as factual as possible on an application, if someone is going to fudge anywhere, it will be here.

The initial job application is also one of your strongest lines of defense, as it offers – voluntarily and willingly – a variety of verifiable information you can use to separate fact from fiction. The following are some simple facts you can verify based on the application alone,

Identity

Having an applicant's proper name and address and the correct spelling of all this information, instantly gives you the tools you need to conduct a thorough "background investigation" of sorts. You can also verify that the identity provided is, in fact, accurate to avoid missing possible adverse findings. For instance, by using the applicant's name, you can search for any past criminal convictions, including:

- **Misdemeanors:** A minor crime, punishable by fine or confinement in a local jail or county correctional facility other than prison. (Examples include: petit larceny, DWI, assault, and battery.)
- **Felonies:** A serious crime that is punishable by more than one year of imprisonment up to death by execution. (Examples include: rape, murder, burglary, and serious drug-related offenses!)

Clearly, such a background check can help you determine possible convictions associated with an applicant, and once the proper process is followed, you can determine if that person is a proper fit for your company.

Discriminatory practices or arbitrarily not hiring someone based upon a conviction is no longer an option in the United States, nor should it be. Instead, an employer must consider a number of factors before making an adverse hiring decision. We will cover more of that later.

Residence History

Knowing an applicant's residence history can also provide clues to how stable – or unstable – he might be and also give us some indicators as to where possible adverse findings exist. From my experience, most applicants tend to have adverse findings (convictions) in the areas of residency – so this is very important in the process!

Separate from the adverse finding component, renting isn't a sin. But if the applicant is a chronic renter – moving from apartment to apartment, breaking leases, all within the span of a year or two – it might be a sign of his lack of dedication, commitment or attention to detail.

Conversely, if he owns his house, are his bills paid up? Is there a lien on the property? Several liens? Is a foreclosure imminent? These aren't signs of a bad person, per se, but perhaps one who really needs the job – or simply *a* job. Oftentimes the applicant can explain such discrepancies easily.

For instance, in the wake of the real estate bubble bursting many applicants may have shoddy resident histories and less than glowing financial records, but taken into consideration with the rest of your informal background information, the evidence could lead to one too many red flag for you to consider hiring.

Motor Vehicle Operator's License

Obtaining an applicant's driver's license information – ID #, address, and photo ID,– is another host of information that can prove useful as you dig deeper into his background.

As a matter of fact, in many states, a Motor Vehicle Operator's License Search will reveal many infractions/ scofflaws that could be indicative of larger issues. Generally, first time DWI/DWAI offenses as well as Marijuana Possession (small quantities) would only be identified by conducting such a search.

In addition, it provides the following for both research purposes and to have on record in case of trouble later on:

- **Photo ID:** What the applicant looked like at the time of hire
- **Vehicle(s):** What vehicle(s) were registered to the applicant at the time of hire
- **Address:** Current residence at time of hire

While this may seem like paltry stuff at first glance, it can prove useful later on during a workers' comp claim when the employee changes his story. There is your information, right there in his employee file!

To that end, data collection – as much information as you can gather, in as many physical forms – should be an increasing part of your Defensive Hiring Strategy from day one.

Education/Degree Verification

If there is one area of a resume and/or application that is most often and regularly falsified or in many cases, "mis-remembered," it is either the education or degree received, where it was received or when it was received. With technology being what it is today, these credits are quickly and easily verified – and should be done so.

Credit

You have to be careful with running an applicant's credit report, particularly in certain states such as California, Colorado, Illinois and Maryland, where it is illegal to use credit reports as a means to make an employment decision.

Credit interpretation leaves a lot to be desired in the realm of making a hard and fast employment decision. Unfortunately, there are no clear-cut methods to objectively consider one's credit history in light of an employment process which can lead you down a rocky road. The laws are constantly changing throughout the United States so if you pursue this course, ensure that you are following the proper state requirements!

However, an alternative exists to give you much of the same information in an objective manner; and that is in checking on whether or not a job applicant has ever had bankruptcies, liens and/or judgments against him. These past financial discrepancies can often indicate major "red flags" that would be issues in a hiring decision and report similar information as credit, but non-discriminatory and non-invasive.

Employment History

Be sure to check the applicant's employment history for various other red flags, particularly when it comes to productivity and performance. For instance, are there big gaps in employment and are the applicant's explanations for them reasonable enough to satisfy you? Did the application indicate what his title was in each prior employment and ensure that verification is made! Was the employee prone to workplace injuries in/on his previous job(s)? This can indicate how safe the applicant was at his previous job, and whether or not his injuries ever lead to lost or missed time at work. Be careful though; workplace injuries and workers' comp claims history are not legal to search in all states in an employment decision.

References

Another area of the application to look closely at is the reference responses. For instance, is there any information here that can help in a potential investigation later on? For example, if a reference indicates that they worked with the applicant in the past, try to make a note in the personnel file and give to investigators at the appropriate time.

Oftentimes what you're looking for, from a defensive position in case the hire evolves into a workers' comp situation, is any evidence, support or proof that the applicant has a history of *behavior* that might have contributed to being careless, lazy or indifferent on the job.

Things like references and past employers, as well as the real reason why they separated employment, can be helpful in that regard. So can job-hopping, or not staying at one employer for an extended period of time, which can demonstrate a lack of stability, maturity, and respect for workplace conditions.

Personal Affiliations/Associations

While most of this "hunting and gathering" of information has so far been focused on the professional, don't neglect the personal aspect of an applicant's life as well. Such information can be particularly useful in both predicting a successful hire as well as providing background information for a future investigation.

For instance:

- **What sports or hobbies does the applicant enjoy doing?** Maybe he's a big football fan. This might mean a good cultural fit for the organization, on one hand, or potential valuable information for an investigation on the other. For instance, oftentimes when doing investigations for workers' comp allegations or insurance fraud, knowing what outside interests an employee has can point us in the right direction for finding fraud. They might be playing tag football with their buddies every weekend despite filing for disability leave, or attending every home game of their local sports team while still claiming emotional distress.

- **Who are the applicant's emergency contacts, references and close friends?** Knowing whom the applicant hangs out with, personally, professionally, casually and on a family level, can prove helpful in an investigation later on.

Again, such information may appear trivial as part of the hiring process, but can prove absolutely essential if the employee ever makes a fraudulent workers' comp claim.

Social Networking Presence

One big aid in both determining a good from a bad hire and aiding workers' comp or fraud investigations later is the presence of applicants on various social networking sites, such as Facebook, Twitter, Tumblr, Instagram and elsewhere and they continue to evolve daily.

It should be the task of every human resource department to outsource this process to do an initial search of the top five to ten social media sites using the applicant's information to see how he presents himself outside of office hours. This process must be done so very carefully and in accordance with the State and Federal Laws surrounding the use of any potential information found. Remember, applicants are entitled to many rights so discriminatory practices are not permitted, but prudence and a solid process is!

This is a great way to test for organizational fit, and even appropriateness. For instance, you might run a Christian Education Publisher and be considering an applicant for a new editor who, by all means, looks great on paper. That is until you check her out on Facebook and see that she parties all night, curses like a sailor and has trashed her last three employers viciously all over Facebook and Twitter!

There are certain non-discriminatory patterns you have to look out for, but over and above those – check with HR first – be sure to monitor behavior of new and even old hires regularly to ensure not only that you are keeping abreast of any "red flag" issues in behavior but also preparing a case against future workers' comp claims.

Parting Words

Hopefully by now you can see the wide variety of options available to you when planning a Defensive Hiring Protocol in your own organization. Whether you use some of the available options, or all of them, is up to you, the culture of your organization, your own personality and, I suppose, your risk tolerance.

My feeling is that if you've ever been burned by a workers' comp claim in the past, you'll want to use all of them – and anymore you can come up with on your own. But regardless of which specific and particular strategies you use, the real goal is to do something before you make a bad hire – to prevent a poor fit as well as trouble down the road.

You'd be amazed by how many companies simply sit, hope and wait that "nothing bad will happen," as if the fate of their entire organization can be left to chance. As we saw in the earliest portions of this very chapter, bad, wrong, quick or careless hires contribute to the shutting down of one-third of this country's businesses every year.

Don't let yours become yet another statistic. Instead, put a strategy in place – now, sooner rather than later – to ensure that you are doing your very best due diligence to prevent one bad hire from turning into a workers comp nightmare.

CHAPTER 2

Preventive Maintenance Through Human Resources

Traditionally speaking, in most organizations, the role of HR ends the minute a new employee is hired and they slide his or her (mostly blank) file into the cabinet drawer.

But in today's modern world of increasing – and increasingly costly – workers' comp claims and other issues of fraud and abuse, HR needs to take an expanded role and be part of what I call the "preventive maintenance" of a company's ongoing battle against fraud in all forms.

In the last chapter, we focused on how HR can wage a preemptive strike against hiring a bad employee through a background check, closer scrutiny and general "pulse taking" about whether or not a prospect is a good fit for the organization. In this chapter, we'll see how giving HR an expanded role – and priority – in the company will help everyone become part of what I call the overall "Risk Mitigation Strategy."

Train, Train and Train Some More: *Honing Your Risk Mitigation Strategy*

I introduced the concept of having a Risk Mitigation Strategy in the last chapter and will reinforce it here, and throughout the book. If you don't have a strategy, then you are simply unprepared for the risk of a claim down the line – and it will end up costing you big.

And while HR should be at the core of this strategy, everyone should be involved. And I do mean everyone. You may have seen in the news recently where a couple of base jumpers were able to infiltrate security at the new World Trade Center site, climb to the top of New York's highest tower and literally jump off the roof – without intervention from a single employee on premises. As one jumper told *The New York Times* after his arrest, "We just kind of walked in..."

From an investigative standpoint I can't even begin to tell you, legally and financially, how costly this could be for the company that manages the building in terms of liability.

It can be no less costly for you if, say, a visitor to your building trips and falls, or a vendor injures himself while on premises or a new employee can claim he wasn't properly trained in how to safely operate a machine, etc.

Training your staff in an overall risk mitigation strategy is crucial, and starts from HR to fan outward throughout the entire organization. Will everyone play as crucial a role to risk mitigation as HR and your appointed risk manager? Not very likely, but the more "hands on deck" when it comes to mitigating risk, the less costly it will be when risk rears its ugly head.

Let's say you run a toy factory and HR has just cleared a new factory line worker to start on Monday morning. We'll call him "Joe." Joe shows up to work on Monday morning, not really knowing where to go.

He winds up in the reception area right at 9 AM, where a busy secretary instructs Joe to go to HR, who looks up his file, finds out he's in production and sends him to the factory floor. Before even meeting his direct supervisor, Joe trips over a new shipment of widgets, lands on his elbow, shatters his forearm and spends the next two days in the hospital, the next two weeks recovering, and the next two months rehabbing...all on the company dime without working a single shift.

The fall, and the subsequent cost to the organization, could have all been avoided by a simple "chain of command" as the most rudimentary part of the Risk Mitigation Strategy.

For instance, in a more risk averse scenario, the scene could have played out like this: "Joe" might have walked into the main reception area and been greeted by an informed receptionist who, as part of the Risk Mitigation Strategy knows her role and has been trained to have every visitor to the office sign in and receive a visitor or employee badge.

Once "badged," Joe could have been directed to his direct supervisor in production, rather than straight to the factory floor. Here he could receive both proper orientation and training – and sign off on both – before proceeding to the factory floor and his role in the production process. This doesn't even take into consideration the fact that Joe could be a person that was hired by a competitor or outside firm to infiltrate information. While on site, what if Joe happened to steal sensitive information, or better yet, launch an attack on the IT infrastructure or proprietary information of the organization causing significant security concerns as well as data breaches?

The two scenarios couldn't be any more opposite. The only major difference between them is the training involved in making every staff member a part of the Risk Mitigation Strategy.

Many companies complain of the cost of all this extra work, but the main cost is in educating your people, and the rewards are avoiding potentially hundreds of thousands of dollars in losses from losing a comp claim case.

In the scenario with "Joe" above there were no extra people hired on to make the organization safer, merely educating people to be extra vigilant about taking an extra step or two to observe, inform and direct a new employee, visitor or vendor.

The receptionist simply needed to ask a question, provide an answer, ask Joe to sign in, give him a badge and perhaps escort him to meet his direct supervisor. The badge let other employees know Joe was "okay" and had passed through one layer of the Risk Mitigation Strategy. Joe's direct supervisor would have had to train him anyway, so really the cost in this scenario was nil – but the benefits immeasurable.

Finally, training is a part of the cost of doing business. Nearly every new employee needs to be trained to some degree, some to a fairly lengthy degree. Consider our machinist, Joe; it will likely take him a week or more to be fully trained in his position until he is fluent. Why aren't we training everyone on our staff to be part of our Risk Mitigation Strategy as well?

Being Proactive is the Key to Prevention

In addition to training, part of preventive maintenance – again, starting with HR and branching out to the rest of the organization, from top to bottom – is maintaining vigilance while being alert to potential problems on the horizon.

HR, leadership, management, team members, coworkers, colleagues and even reports from other teams can all be vigilant when it comes to red flags about a potentially problematic employee.

In fact, such employees typically count on others to see only "part of the puzzle" and hence get away with schemes, frauds or simply negligence for far longer as opposed to being observed by everyone all at once.

For instance, as typically happens in organizations, an employee – we'll call her "April" – is able to slip through the cracks merely because the left hand doesn't know what the right hand is doing.

Here's how it works: April typically calls into work either on a Friday or a Monday to score herself an extra three-day weekend, every other week or so. Regularly missed work costs both April and her team loss of productivity and momentum, and the company loss of profits.

April is savvy enough to call someone different every time, one manager here, another manager there, a coworker here, another coworker there, so that it takes awhile for folks to look up and say, "Hey, April's not here again?"

When everyone puts the facts together – "Hey, she was out this Friday, that Monday, another Friday, another Monday," etc. – it's clear that this is a problem employee with little to no dedication or motivation, and for that matter, not much to offer the team/company. Meanwhile, she's gotten away with "robbing" the company of time off for six or seven months.

Such scenarios can be avoided, or at least mitigated, by managing risk in the following ways:

- **Keep a disciplinary log:** Disciplinary logs are critical in not only protecting your organization from fraud but identifying problem employees and cutting them loose before that ever happens. If it was standard operating procedure to record all employee absences in every department in one central location such as HR, her manager(s) – and their manager(s) – could have discovered her reckless behavior much earlier and solved the problem immediately. The same holds true for any disciplinary action, infraction, conflict or resolution.

- **Performance evaluations:** Consider doing more than annual evaluations for your employees, but 90-day evaluations. This allows everyone involved to report on employee behavior and not let a year of unproductive, unmotivated, unprofitable behavior to continue.

- **Identify risk factors to evaluate:** Evaluations are critical, but less so without identifying specific risk factors to evaluate. These will vary from industry to industry, and even company to company. They shouldn't be ignored. For instance, if you're in the construction industry, it's important to determine if a worker has been cited in the last ninety days. Perhaps they did not wear their hardhat, did not report a work-related incident, or were careless. These risk factors are virtual "red flags" to management/leadership because they could clearly lead to bigger issues later.

- Infinity Screening: While an initial background check before hiring is good, many companies stop there and never dig into current employee behaviors, backgrounds or potential problems. Infinity, or annual background checks help organizations like yours "recheck" employees annually to ensure that they have not slipped into any challenges.

The thing to remember here is that risk assessment is an ongoing, habitual behavior. In much the same way as your computer runs virus protection scans regularly – or should – you should be following your Risk Mitigation Strategy to ensure that your organization is safe from fraudulent workers' comp claims as well

Red Flags: *They Only Help if You Notice Them*

Part of your ongoing training, strategy and overall risk management "mindset" should include being ever vigilant of a laundry list of red flags. These help identify an employee who has questionable ethics or little organizational loyalty, that left unchecked, could lead to a fraudulent workers' comp claim. Some of these red flags include:

- **The Crisis Addict:** What's encouraging about risk mitigation is that if you make it a habit and a strategy, certain indicators will quickly become clear and patterns will start to emerge. One is the "crisis addict," and there is usually one in every organization (often more than one). This is the person who, for whatever reason, always has an emergency, crisis or extenuating circumstance where they are out for a day, a week, or weeks at a time. The problem is they are just smart enough to use legitimate – or legitimate-sounding – excuses, but not quite disciplined enough to space them out often enough. So one week her mother might be in the hospital. The next her husband tripped and fell, or her kid might be sick, or an aunt or a cousin is ill, and she has to care for them and on and on it goes.

- **Transportation Troubles.** Another red flag we often see in investigations is when the employee has constant trouble with transportation. Their own car is always breaking down, they need to borrow someone's car, or they need rides to and from work. Yet, they do not avail themselves of the ample public transportation that is available. The question then becomes, *why don't they have a car?* Do they have a DUI/DWI they didn't tell you about? Is it recent, old, or ongoing? Do they even possess a valid Operator's License?
- **Attendance.** Attendance is a big issue and one we need to be ever vigilant about. Is the employee being regular in his or her attendance? If so, great. If not, why not? How often is he absent from work? Do his excuses jibe? Are there medical excuses? Imperfect, or even reckless attendance can indicate different issues, such as

being unhappy or unsatisfied at work, but just as often they can send up a red flag about an employee's performance and/or ethics.

- **Sick and PTO time.** In the same vein as attendance, you also need to be wary of employees who know exactly how to "game the system" and get the most out of their sick and paid time off (PTO) hours. Look for "spikes" of activity as well. For instance, there tends to be an average of how the majority of employees use their sick, paid and leave time. When a particular employees fall outside that norm – and often *well* outside that norm – be wary.

- **Leaves of Absence.** Once sick and PTO time is used, be familiar with what your organization's policy is and be sure to conduct routine assessments. Does FMLA or ADA Apply? Have you considered the "reasonable accommodation" clause, and if it is not met, what are your repercussions? What will you do if the employee is not satisfied with what is granted or not granted? This could lead to other possible claims, including an alleged injury at work the following week. Conduct assessments of leave requests to determine possible patterns of behavior that could lead to a claim later. Leave of Absence that is not managed properly, or where red flags are ignored, can lead to more costly, significant issues for an organization later.

- **Claim activity – past, present and future.** Any type of claim should raise an automatic red flag, not because all claims are faulty, but because claims are out of the ordinary and should be treated as such. In particular, a claim that happens over the weekend but doesn't get reported until Monday, or frequent claims that increase in severity should set off red flags that the employee should be monitored.

- **Point of contact.** Something as simple as where the employee gets paid – or how – can be a vital red flag that should be monitored if raised. If there are constant change of address requests to HR about where to send payment, or the addresses don't match up to personal information provided at the time of application – which would only be spotted in a follow-up or "recheck" background check – that could be a red flag that your employee is involved in questionable ethics and/or behavior and needs to be monitored throughout the length of employment.

- **Monitor cross-management behaviors.** Having friends in "high places" is how many fraudulent claims get started. It's also how many overworked managers keep the peace. For instance, you can have an employee who's doing a good job and yet still engages in questionable behavior – missed days or late claims – and that manager might not record it or log it or report it because performance is still high. That doesn't mean the red flags aren't there, or that performance won't slip.

- **Sick and PTO time.** Be wary of employees who know exactly how to "game the system" and get the most out of their sick and paid time off, or PTO, hours. Look for "spikes" of activity as well. For instance, there tends to be an average of how the majority of employees use their sick, paid and leave time, and when particular employees fall outside that norm – and often well outside that norm – be wary. For instance, someone using up their sick or PTO time in a matter of, say, weeks or less than two months, versus the majority of employees who take six months to a year to use the same amount of days, should send off a huge red flag.

Taken individually, each of these red flags can be worth noting, but if, when and as they start to add up, action needs to be taken sooner than later. Fortunately, with an active Risk Mitigation Strategy and an ongoing "preventative" mindset about the HR, risk team and entire organization, that is easier done than said.

Parting Words

Ultimately, having a Risk Mitigation Strategy in place, as well as constant and vigilant monitoring, will ensure that you are practicing preventive maintenance through, but not solely relying on, the Human Resources department.

You can't always avoid risk, but you can certainly mitigate some. Nothing I've suggested here is either unreasonable or, for that matter, unattainable. It doesn't take a ton of manpower, hours or money to be constantly watchful against employee fraud; it only takes a little extra effort and due-diligence spread out across the entire organization.

CHAPTER 3

Incident, Risk & Liability

Workplace incidents happen to the best of us, and are never pleasant – for the employee or the employer. The goal of this book is to provide sound guidance and structure around how to best avoid an incident in the first place and, when and if one happens, mitigate the loss to you and your company.

To that end, we have previously discussed *What Employers Should Do **Before** a Hiring Decision is Made* and *Preventive Maintenance Through Human Resources*. Now it's time to address what happens before, during and after an actual workplace incident occurs.

Understanding Your Experience Modification Rating (MOD)

Let's start by understanding your experience modification rating, more commonly referred to as your "MOD." Like individuals, companies must get insurance to protect themselves in case of a work-related accident, or incident.

In this case, they must obtain workers' comp insurance. And as with all insurance, the more claims made in the past, the higher the cost obtaining – and keeping – insurance will be.

NCCI, the nation's most comprehensive source of workers' compensation insurance information, explains MOD this way: "In workers' compensation experience rating, the actual payroll and loss data of the individual employer is analyzed over a period of time. In general, an employer with better-than-average loss experience receives a credit, while an employer with worse-than-average experience carries a debit rating. Experience rating takes the average loss experience and modifies it based on the individual's own loss experience." [**Source**: www.ncci.com]

In this case, "loss experience" refers to losses incurred by the company due to a workers' comp claim. In other words, the fewer incidents you have on site, the more favorable (lower) your MOD rating is going to be; the more incidents you have, the less favorable (higher) the rating will be.

It's just like car insurance. If you have an "incident" every few months, or even weeks, where you're in a fender bender and are constantly calling your insurance agent to make yet another claim, your insurance is going to go up… and up and up and up.

Conversely, there are safe drivers out there who go years – decades, even – without making a single claim who get favorable "safe driver" discounts as their insurance continues to go down.

That is why mitigating your risks is so mission critical when it comes to workers' compensation insurance. Even with a low MOD rating, workers' comp insurance isn't cheap. An incident or two at your company could affect your MOD rating so adversely that the jump in price of your new, higher insurance could make the difference between the company succeeding or, quite literally, going out of business.

How to Keep Your MOD Rating Low

We all know accidents will happen; that's why they're called accidents. But doing your best to mitigate the risk of such incidents can help avoid them now and in the future.

One way to positively affect your MOD rating is to track incidents carefully and act immediately to rectify whatever situation(s) contributed to the incident in the first place. Even small claims can affect your MOD rating; tracking, rectifying and avoiding future incidents can help keep your MOD rating – and your insurance costs – low.

As Retailers Mutual Insurance Company warns, "One of the most important things you can do to reduce your mod from year to year is to improve workplace safety and reduce claims. The severity and frequency of your claims directly impact whether your MOD rises or falls from year to year. Some analysts believe that a history of small, recurring claims can have a greater negative impact on your mod than one large claim. Why? Because it suggests that a continuing problem exists at your business. Which is why you need to pay special attention to repeat accidents." [**Source**: www. retailersmutual.com]

Another thing you can do to get the most favorable workers' comp insurance rates available is to find an insurance broker who not only understands workers' comp but knows your industry as well and knows the best carriers that work with your industry regularly. This will help to pair you with the right insurance for your needs, both now and in the future.

How to Document an Incident

When and if an incident does occur, it helps to document it both quickly and properly. While it's best to avoid an accident altogether – see Chapters 1 and 2 of this book – proper documentation, processing and treatment can help reduce the effects of an accident should one occur and, hopefully, help the company learn and avoid the next one.

The following is some helpful advice provided by the New York State Workers' Compensation Board. They provide simple steps for how best to document an incident should one occur:

- The first step is to immediately notify the employee's supervisor and get him or her involved.
- The next step would be to document the accident using whatever forms are appropriate for your company.
- At the same time, steps must be taken to provide the employee with immediate and appropriate medical treatment. Swift action here will ensure that the employee's needs are immediately met and that a minor injury doesn't turn into a major one.
- The next step would be a full investigation – with proper documentation – into the incident. How did it happen? Who was there to see it? What factors contributed to the incident? The

investigation process is critical to determining who was at fault, and to what degree the company is responsible (see the next section for more on this process).

- Determine whether the incident is "minor" incident, or if there is more involved. If minor, which the New York State Workers' Compensation Board describes as "requiring two or fewer treatments by a person rendering first aid, and with lost time of less than one day beyond the end of the working shift on which the accident occurred," the employer may choose to pay for first aid treatments directly. This method is commonly used by larger employers who participate in the claims process early on to help mitigate the overall exposure. This can often be cheaper than filing, and paying, a claim. If an incident is determined to be more involved than described above, it must be reported to your local Workers' Compensation Board and your insurance carrier. [**Source**: www.wcb.ny.gov]

As you can see, the steps are fairly straightforward and clear. Unfortunately, since incidents are the exception rather than the norm, many companies don't have a plan in place, or system, for reporting them.

Is the Injury Type Compensable?

Once the incident has been thoroughly reported, investigated and documented, the next step is to determine whether or not the employee should be compensated for his or her injuries. This issue boils down

The Claim Game

to the simple question of whether or not the claim is a work-related injury.

What determines a work-related injury? According to FindLaw.com, "A work-related injury is one that happened while you were doing something on behalf of your employer or otherwise in the course of employment. Most injuries that can be classified as work-related are those that occur at the workplace, but also may occur in company-owned trucks and other locations as long as the employee was doing something connected to his or her job. This includes company parties and other social events sponsored by an employer, but not necessarily on company-owned property."

As you might imagine, the implications of whether or not an injury was "work related" are fairly broad, and open to interpretation on a state by state basis.

How to Investigate an Incident

For the sake of this next section, let's assume that a.) You have had an incident at work and b.) It has been determined it was a work-related injury and is therefore compensable (i.e., the employee is entitled to compensation).

In such a case, it is imperative that you conduct a thorough investigation promptly as time is of the essence. As part of your investigation, follow the basic steps below as promptly, and as thoroughly, as possible:

- **Get witness statements:** With every day that passes, the investigation erodes just a little more. Witnesses who were there that day forget times, and specifics. Some get fired or move away and are never quite as invested as you are in separating fact from fiction. And yet their contributions to the investigation can't be underestimated.

- **Determine the area of investigation:** What factors are you going to focus on in the investigation? Was the incident on-site or off-site? Who interacted with the employee before, during and after the incident and what can they tell you about what might have contributed to it? For instance, perhaps you have determined that drinking was involved as part of the incident. Maybe the employee has a history of drinking on the job, as supported by documentation of times he had been written up. Maybe one or more witnesses claim he was drinking at the time of the incident, or just before. It may still be a work-related incident and the employee may still be compensable, but having the facts as a result of the investigation might help to lessen the payout. Therefore, this is obviously an area that needs to be delved into further, and likely should become the area, or locus, of the investigation.

- **Launch an ongoing social media investigation:** It's amazing what folks will share on social media these days, perhaps assuming no one at work will ever see what is posted. This is why social media (which is ever-changing) – Instagram, Facebook, Twitter, Tumblr, YouTube, etc. – should become an immediate ongoing part of your investigation. Learning that someone who is claiming they might need multiple months of recovery time from their work related incident is out water skiing or taking in a theme park, or even talking about how they'll spend their award money, can play a crucial role in the workers' comp investigation.

- **Review the employee's HR folder:** There may also be clues to uncover in the employee's HR folder. Recall the pre-hiring stage, and the information you hopefully gathered including contact information, driver's license and previous employment. There may be also on-the-job issues such as disciplinary reports, write-ups, performance evaluations and the like. Did the employee have frequent absences, medical or other issues? All of this can contribute toward the employee's frame of mind, performance and future with the company at the time of the incident. It is also important that any minor or major workers' comp incident paperwork become a part of the employee's HR file to avoid, prevent or mitigate future incidents as well.

- **Move with confidence and speed:** These investigations need to be quiet, quick and confidential. I've seen many instances where an employee may have multiple family members working on the same job site and. if an investigation isn't carried out carefully, quickly and confidentially, word gets out, influences are made and investigations hampered because of a lack of cooperation. Your actions are being monitored by all stakeholders so having a solid proactive approach will help you set the tone.

I can't say enough about the importance of conducting a thorough, confidential and complete investigation centered on the incident in question. Not only is this imperative to mitigate and hopefully lessen the cost associated with the claim and eventual payout, such investigations ultimately help prevent future injuries as well.

Determine the Nature of the Injury

Once the dust has settled, the claim has been filed, and an investigation is completed – or is ongoing – it is time to enter into the determination phase of the incident. In other words, you must determine the nature of the injury. Specifically, is it a short-term, long-term, partial or permanent injury?

Short-term injury

Short-term injuries can mean the worker is out for a few shifts, to a few days to a few weeks. This could mean finding a replacement for those shifts within the existing employee pool or hiring a temporary worker to cover those shifts. Both require some careful planning, time and resource management as well as full budgetary considerations.

Long-term injury

Long-term injuries may mean the claimant is out for a few months up to a year. This type of injury typically can't be covered with existing employees covering shifts for multiple months, and usually requires a full-time, temporary replacement to cover the loss. This is on top of paying out a claim for the injured worker.

Many employers hold off on conducting an investigation until they determine whether the injury is short- or long-term. My suggestion is to err on the side of caution and conduct an investigation regardless of the nature of the injury.

I've seen many instances where, for instance, an employee might have a back injury that he says will "only keep me out for a day or two." Fair enough, but what if the pain persists and becomes chronic? What if some particularly litigious or opportunistic family member convinces him that he could ride a full claim for months, or even years?

It happens, a lot more often than you might think, and the only way to fight a fraudulent claim is with a quick response, a thorough investigation and plenty of paperwork to back it all up.

Partial injury

A partial injury might mean that the employee can take some time off, heal and return to work with little to no effect on his work. He might use the other hand for a few weeks, or sit on a stool next to the assembly line. She might be able to work a different machine for a few weeks before regaining full strength and returning to her regular job. All of these implications are important for you, as the employer, to consider when determining the nature of a workers' comp injury.

Permanent injury

Finally, permanent injuries will transport you, as the employer, to the world of long-term disability and all that that entails.

Obviously, the answers to these questions have a direct bearing on the amount of time, energy, resources and money you will have to spend to either cover the employee's absence or replace him or her altogether.

Steps for Moving Forward

Once you have conducted a thorough investigation and assessed the nature of the injury, it is time to move forward into the next phase of the post-claim process. This phase requires a variety of moving parts.

Legal

What are your legal responsibilities, liabilities and options in the wake of the incident? It's finally time to get the lawyers involved to determine exactly where you stand and to hopefully project realistic costs associated with the claim in the future.

Costs

Another aspect of this part of the claim review is to determine how much the claim might cost you and how to pay for it. What reserves do you have on tap for out of pocket costs, if any?

How will the claim, if paid out by the insurance carrier, affect your MOD or future payments? What will the employee's prolonged absence cost you in terms of overtime for the employees covering his shifts or a temp worker? Knowing what costs are involved will help you prepare for them fully.

Return to Work Program

If the injury is determined to be short-term and/or partial, or even long-term, you should work with HR to begin a Return to Work, or RTW, program. This might include the aid of a nurse or a physical therapist. There should also be a timeline for the employee to return to work, such as in six days, two months, four months, etc.

Or, will the employee ever return to work? They may be able to, but might have decided they no longer want to. All of this requires active participation, measurement and monitoring to determine how it affects you, as the employer.

Ultimately, the goal of any RTW program is two-fold: either get the employee back to work safely and in a reasonable timeline or determine the employee can't, or won't, return to work and settle the claim. Implementing and maintaining a realistic RTW program will help accomplish either goal.

Post-Incident Care

Next up, determine what care the employee might need, post-incident. This may mean having a nurse assigned to the employee's care to ensure he or she is getting full treatment for issues related to the accident. This can help keep the employee on track for his RTW program, determine if and when that might happen, or even if it won't happen.

A qualified nurse case manager can help with monitoring and measuring the employee's progress and continually update HR about said progress.

Conduct an Independent Medical Exam

An Independent Medical Exam, or IME, is the employer's and the insurance carrier's opportunity to independently conduct an exam of the employee to see for themselves, how severe the injury might be. This can be helpful in making sense of the various timelines being floated by the insurance carrier, the employee's physician/team and even the employee himself. Depending on each state, there are some statutory requirements for IMEs at various intervals throughout the claims process, however I would encourage an IME at regular intervals especially if the claimant does not appear to be interested (or able) to return to work, even "light duty."

Monitor and Measure

I'm a firm believer in monitoring and measuring every part of the claims process, from beginning to end and, as you saw in the book's first two chapters... even before the beginning! One part of the monitoring process is determining if further investigation is needed or, if you haven't done one, if AN investigation is needed.

For instance, in the terms of a so-called "minor" injury, you might have an employee who injures his hand on a piece of machinery and it doesn't appear too major. He says, "Listen, it's Friday, just give me the weekend off, let me heal and I'll be back to work on Monday, no worries." If you don't make a claim right there, report the injury, send him to the emergency room or at least the nurse, write it up, or log it, what's to prevent him from going home over the weekend and thinking it over... to his advantage?

Now he comes back Monday morning, claiming the injury is way worse than he thought, plus it's aggravated an existing neck injury he used to have. He may need weeks, even months, to recover and, oh yeah, he's brought an attorney and so on.

Monitoring the situation and launching an investigation first thing and keeping tabs on it – measuring – is your own professional line of defense and protection against workers' comp fraud.

Classification and Permanency

It is also during the post-incident phase where a classification occurs to determine the clinical extent of the injury. Is it, in fact, a permanent disability as determined by your local Workers' Compensation Board? Or is there hope of the employee returning to work with a partial, or short-term, injury?

In terms of permanent injury, one term you'll want to be familiar with is whether or not the employee has reached what's known as Maximized Medical Improvement, or MMI. As the name implies, this is a determination by medical professionals that the employee's health is as good as they're going to get, and will never get any better.

As defined by New York Workers' Compensation Defense, "Often times the Independent Medical

Examiner will opine the claimant has reached MMI and there is a permanent disability. The claimant is then directed by the Board to produce their own permanency report and their treating physician(s) opine the claimant has not yet reached MMI. The issue then has to be litigated and a WC Law Judge determines whether the claimant has reached MMI." [**Source**: www. nyworkerscompensationdefense.com]

For instance, let's say a 38-year-old employee has suffered a back injury at your plant and both a medical professional and your local Workers' Compensation Board/Judge has determined that the employee has reached MMI and that the injury is a permanent one. There is a cost to be determined around that employee based on his age, amount he could have expected to earn annually, or the amount of years he might have worked, which all need to be factored into the insurance claim and determined before a judgment for compensation is made. Classification is critical to determining how much will be paid out by your insurance carrier.

Schedule Loss of Use Award (SLU)

Another factor to consider is the schedule loss of use award, or SLU. As defined by the New York State Workers Compensation Board, the SLU is "A Schedule Loss of Use award (known as an SLU), an additional cash payment. It pays you for an injury that leaves you with less ability in a body part than you had before the injury. If you don't get back the same level of use in the injured body part, because you now have a permanent disability, you may be eligible for an SLU payment." [**Source**: www. wcb.ny.gov]

In other words, each state has a standard way of measuring – according to a specific schedule – the value of each injury, permanent or non-permanent, short-term or long-term. Whether the loss of a limb, a back injury, chronic pain, nerve damage, or vision or hearing loss, each injury has its own net worth to be determined by the appropriate parties.

So depending on your state and certain allowances given the SLU, your award will be determined by averaging the classification of the injury, times the percentage of use you still have, or lost, as a result of that injury, time lost on the job, your current salary and a multiple of allowable weeks to determine the eventual award.

Ongoing Efforts

Finally, it's important to never quite drop the matter completely. That is, until a claim is settled. If you have an employee and the claim is ongoing-they haven't settled or the courts haven't determined a settlement yet-stay on the investigation as if it's open, active and a top priority.

Monitor those social media accounts to ensure that the employee isn't out there jet skiing or boogie boarding or bragging about how he's taking your company for a ride.

This is not to say that you shouldn't be empathetic with a valid claim, and do all you can to ensure a long, healthy life for your injured employee. But over and above that, there is simply no reason not to protect yourself by keeping the investigation open and actively monitoring the situation to insure your own best interests are being protected.

Let Your Employees Help You... Help Them

One way to move forward with confidence is to include your employees as part of your eyes, ears and continual monitoring program. Coworkers do not like fraudulent colleagues, nor do they like to pick up the slack for the "fraudsters.' Don't do it all alone, or even leave it up to your HR department to handle everything themselves.

As part of the company, employees have both the right and the responsibility to be a part of the workplace safety discussion. That means that prevention is up to them as well, and as you and your organization continue to measure and monitor ongoing safety issues, your employees can be a valuable part of the process.

Here are some simple ways you can let your employees help you... to help them:

- Make it as easy as possible for your people to report an injury immediately after it happens. Drill the process and procedure from their first day on the job and regularly throughout their employment so there is never a doubt about what the first step is after an injury – or how to accomplish it.
- Have a standard "injury treatment form" that employees must bring with them to their treating physician. Work with HR, legal and corporate to make sure it contains all the data needed to support your preventive measures at work and provide all the information necessary during an ongoing investigation.

- One thing to monitor and measure with employees is how they are progressing in their recovery – or even IF they are progressing Schedule regular meetings to assess their RTW status.
- Record all steps of the process by having employees sign off on various forms stating not only what part of the process they are in – reporting the injury, getting it treated, recovery, post-recovery, or RTW – but also that they acknowledge and understand the process as well.
- Get – and stay – involved in the employee's recovery. Make yourself, or a representative, available if need be for the employee's ongoing medical treatment, hospital or rehab visits.
- Have a policy in place (see previous section) for the employee's RTW. This will streamline the process, for this employee and every employee to follow, and ensure that everything is being done to ensure a fair and just policy for both you and your employees.
- Have an incentive plan in place to better manage workplace injuries and increase overall accountability throughout the organization.

Making your employees part of the reportage and recovery process gives them ownership of their own recovery, and helps you have more eyes and ears to monitor and measure the recovery process itself.

Parting Words

Ultimately, all of this is leading up to one thing: money. The more you document everything, plan ahead, make the workplace safe, play solid defense before hiring your people, have contingencies in place and train your people well, the less incidents you'll have.

The above steps should work to reduce incidents. However, when you do have incidents, the same mindset will help mitigate claims by acting promptly, professionally and with a thorough investigation designed to protect yourself, your assets and your company.

Remember, there are two main options after any incident:

- **Option 1:** Have the employee return to work, healthy and happy
- **Option 2:** Settle the claim sooner rather than later

Obviously, Option 1 is the ideal but, if forced into Option 2, it's critical that your investigation is thorough and complete to minimize damage and/or combat a fraudulent claim.

CHAPTER 4

Investigations 101

Few work-related matters can be as challenging as a workers' comp investigation, but if you find yourself in need of conducting one, hiding your head in the sand or shirking your duties can cost you and your company millions of dollars as a result.

The basics of investigation include not just how to investigate, but what steps to follow and even when to start following them. So many of my clients are unsure of how much they should be doing to investigate, and when to start.

We want to make sure that you have all the tools you need at your disposal to avoid huge claims. Conducting thorough, timely investigations is at the top of that list.

This chapter will focus on what I like to call Investigations 101. Everything you need to know, from when to request an investigation, strategies for defense, the top ten indicators of fraud and case study examples is included here so that you can be more than prepared for your first – or next – claims investigation.

What is Fraud?

Before we begin to investigate fraud, let's make sure we know exactly what it means first. Since my personal

Mario S. Pecoraro

and professional experience is first and foremost in the state of New York, I'll quote from the definition of our New York Code - Article 4, as it defines "Insurance Frauds Prevention":

> **§ 404. Procedures.** * *(a) If the insurance frauds bureau has reason to believe that a person has engaged in, or is engaging in, an act defined in section 155.05 of the penal law, with respect to personal or commercial insurance transactions or section 176.05 of such law, the superintendent may make such investigation within or without this state as he deems necessary to aid in the enforcement of this chapter or to determine whether any person has violated or is about to violate any such provision of the penal law.*

Obviously, this is a legal matter and there are legal considerations to take into account. But over and above what your legal department and/or outside attorneys can do for and with you to aid in an investigation, prevention – and defense – are always up to you.

Why is it Critical to Conduct Fraud and Criminal Investigations?

Again, you may be asking yourself, "Why bother with all this? Why not just pay the claim and get back to work?" I agree; life would be so much easier without the added time, resources, manpower and expense of doing your due diligence in the matters of prevention and then ultimately conducting a fraud investigation.

Conducting an investigation will tell you so much more about a claim and give you inside information on whether or not the claim is even "worth" mitigating. We all know that many claims are NOT fraudulent, but perhaps the claimants are "malingerers." Why let them malinger if that's not necessary, and if there is possible fraud, having some great steps in place early on is key!

However, if you establish yourself as a leader – and a company – who is an "easy payout" for these types of fraudulent or "malingering" employees, you send a message that you're easy pickings and you'll end up spending all your money paying claims – not payroll.

Over and above the threat of continued fraud in your own company, here are some staggering statistics gathered from industry leading sources that tell the larger story of how fraud is affecting companies just like yours all over the country:

- The average medical cost per lost-time claim rose to $28,500 in 2012 from $17,300 ten years earlier. (**Source:** National Council on Compensation Insurance, or NCCI)
- The most frequent types of claims are those where the total size of loss is over $50,000. (**Source:** NCCI)
- The percentage of claims deemed "questionable" (those that are referred to the NICB for closer review and investigation based on one or more indicators of possible fraud) has been steadily rising. National Insurance Crime Bureau. (**Source:** NICB)

- An estimated $80 billion worth of fraudulent claims are made annually in the United States. (**Source:** Coalition Against Insurance Fraud)

As you can see, fraud is more complex, more prevalent and more costly than ever. But it's easy to overlook how fraud affects the country, the marketplace, even your own industry, until you realize how it affects you.

Top 10 Indicators of Fraud

So what are we talking about here? What, exactly, are we looking for? The National Insurance Crime Bureau has identified what it refers to as the **Top 10 Indicators of Fraud**. That is to say, fraudulent comp claims often include one or more of the following ten factors:

- Medical documentation that appears to be altered or fraudulent or a physician's diagnosis inconsistent with the treatment.
- A disgruntled employee, or someone who was slated for a layoff, termination or disciplinary action.
- A new hire or someone with a spotty employment record.
- Accidents or injuries reported to have occurred late Friday or early Monday morning, suggesting it may be the result of a non-work-related, weekend activity.
- An injured worker who is reluctant or refuses to accept treatment from a health care provider.
- A worker who takes off more days than the accident would seem to warrant.

- A delay in reporting an accident.
- An injured worker who is seasonal and about to conclude the job.
- A worker who is observed in work or recreational activities inconsistent with the reported injury.
- An injured employee on a workers' compensation disability who can never be easily contacted or who provides a beeper as his main number. (**Source:** National Insurance Crime Bureau)

Any one of these signs, let alone multiple indicators, should be a "red flag" as to the presence of fraud.

When Is It Time to Launch an Investigation?

Timing is critical when launching an investigation. For my money, sooner is always better, but... how soon is too soon? Investigations can be costly and if you run one every time there is a delay in reporting an incident, for instance, or you hire someone with a spotty work record, you could easily spend the majority of your time investigating your workers rather than training them.

Still, it's important to investigate when appropriate. That's why having a file on every employee – up-to-date, accurate and timely – is mission critical to starting an investigation. In addition to a file that is current, ask yourself:

- Does the employee's medical documentation appear to be altered or fraudulent?
- Is the claim amount over $50,000?
- Is this a seasonal employee who may be looking to win a comp claim before being laid off for the season?

- Is the amount of time the employee has taken off incompatible with his/her type of injury?
- Are they refusing treatment?
- Is this someone who was already slated for a layoff, termination or disciplinary action?
- Did the injury happen late Friday or early Monday morning, suggesting it may be the result of a non-work-related, weekend activity?
- Has there been a delay in reporting an accident?

If you experience more "yes" answers than "no," your antennae should already be up and your gut should be telling you that this matter is at least worth looking into more closely.

Ongoing Investigations: *Social Media and the Digital Age*

Don't forget, there are varying degrees of investigation. Do you need full, 24-hour physical surveillance on an individual? It depends on the severity of the injury, how many indicators of fraud are present and/or the amount of the claim.

You don't want to be spending more on the investigation than you do paying out the claim. However, should you run, say, a simple social media investigation – that can easily be carried out in-house – the minute a claim comes in?

Absolutely.

This type of hands-on, habitual vigilance protects you and your company from fraudulent claims and arms the legal department with information that could potentially short-circuit a costly claim before it ever happens.

Now more than ever, social media is a window into the daily lives of your employees and, since so few of them recognize how transparent their social media accounts may be – Facebook, Twitter, Flickr, Tumblr, etc. – this type of investigation allows you nearly full access to activities that may foil their fraudulent claims.

Let's face it; most employees are not always visible when investigators are out there conducting surveillance, so being proactive to gain other intelligence is critical!

Social Media and Great Pretexting Play Key Roles in the Investigation Process

Such social media searches can reveal the truth about claimant activity levels, can be done on multiple cases to determine if additional investigation is required, and require minimal investment for a great return!

Searches include...

- **Websites**
- **Group Meeting/Scheduling Sites**
- **Photo/Video Sharing Sites**
- **Blogs**
- **Social Network Aggregator Sites**
- **Social Network Sites (General & Career)**
- **Actionable Information & Intelligence**

How soon should you start actively monitoring an employee's social media accounts? For me and my company, a good rule of thumb is to begin when an employee doesn't return to work within thirty days of a work-related incident.

This gives employees a reasonable amount of time to return to work – unless otherwise instructed, in which case you and your team will know this in advance – and give you plenty of time to allow them to do the right thing.

Then again, social media monitoring can reveal a host of fraudulent activities. For instance, while monitoring accounts we've discovered the following:

- One claimant posted about her 5K Race. (In fact, we found the actual race results and the fact that she placed third in her age bracket!)
- Another claimant posted YouTube videos of himself practicing his golf swing!
- Another claimant advertised her "baking" business, and her ability to fulfill orders of all sizes/baked goods (wedding cakes, etc.).

This is where social media provides a window into an individual's activities, and of course fraud and an active investigation can reveal activities that might not otherwise be captured in a more traditional investigation. Although increasingly, social media is becoming an active part of every investigation.

A Word About Pretexts

And it doesn't stop there! Pretext use is becoming a tool that more and more investigative firms are using. A pretext, according to Merriam-Webster is defined as "a purpose or motive alleged or an appearance assumed in order to cloak the real intention or state of affairs."

Many will say that this is an illegal way to secure information, but it's a legal tool that is used often by investigative firms, client permitting, to gain information and intelligence about a subject.

The use of this technique by investigators can be very telling about the level of a claimant's activities. Relatives, neighbors, friends and colleagues when approached utilizing a suitable pretext can be a wealth of information, and the best thing about it is they don't even realize they are helping with the investigation! They can reveal information about a subject's patterns or activities, indicate whether or not they are ever out of the house and can give an investigator a great deal of information!

The Independent Medical Exam, or IME

Before, during and after a workers' comp claim, you are likely to become extremely familiar with the term "IME," which stands for an Independent Medical Exam.

Based on certain statutory regulations in the state in which the claim is being made as well as the employee's prognosis, there is a certain timeline involved in when an IME must be conducted. For instance, if a person doesn't go back to work after so many days and the diagnosis doesn't appear to be getting any better, an IME is scheduled.

This is typically done by the insurance company, but also the best time for you to begin conducting a physical examination of the claimant. Why? Because this is when the employee is forced to tell the doctor all the things they can and can't do, symptoms they are experiencing, why they're not returning to work, and limitations placed upon them by the incident.

If malingering or fraud is going to occur, this is definitely the time to not only stop it – but document it. For instance, if during the IME a claimant tells the physician that they are suffering from extreme back pain but then, on the way home from the doctor's office they swing by their local home improvement store and wrangle a dozen fifty-pound bags of mulch for a big project around the yard, physically documenting that with video or photographic proof is going to seriously refute that claim.

At or around the IME, critical information becomes available to you as the employer, such as:

- Date and time of the IME
- The name and address of the treating physician that will be conducting the IME
- Whether or not the employee needs transportation to the IME
- Information as to claimant's capabilities and restrictions as noted by the physician, but also as stated by the claimant

All of this information, and any other critical data that can be gathered at the time of the IME will be an important addition to the employee's ongoing claim file.

Other important aspects of a claim investigation that is directly medically-related is the claimant's previous medical files. For instance, how are we to know that a claimant doesn't have preexisting conditions that are exacerbating, or even causing, his current condition? How are we to know about recent sports or other injuries that might have affected his work performance or vulnerability to injury?

Making the patient's medical files an early part of the original discovery process is critical in ruling out – or pointing out – any of these contributing medical conditions.

As part of many investigations focused on the medical side of the equation, we will routinely canvas local hospitals, doctor offices or pharmacies looking to gather as much medical information as possible.

The Importance of a Routine Claim Review

It is important to be active, diligent and verbal before, during and after the workers' comp claim. Staying in contact with the claimant, your legal defense team, his legal representation, any and all treating physicians, nurses and rehab workers, for example, is critical to staying on top of the claim and saving yourself tens of thousands of dollars in potential losses.

For instance, after reviewing the claim once the dust has settled and appreciating the parameters of the case, you might reach out to the claimant's counsel and have the following discussion: "Well, the claim is under $50,000, the IME has been conducted, and it's pretty straightforward. If you were to settle for an offer of $12,000 today, we can make this all go away."

Not being diligent about such opportunities, options and offers can be tantamount to literally handing out much more than you might have saved if you had simply engaged in a routine claim review.

Investigation Time: *What to Do When a Claim Comes In*

Now that you've determined that you need to conduct a more thorough, exhaustive claim investigation, how do you start? We've determined when to start, using a simple 30-Day timeline from the date of injury to return to work. But what to do when a claim is actually filed?

Here are ten helpful steps to what to do when a claim comes in:

1. **Have training procedures in place to learn proper injury management and correct post-injury response.** Again, prevention helps not only avoid a claim in the first place but to mitigate losses when and if a claim occurs.

2. **Assign suspicious claims to more experienced adjusters.** Don't leave a claim to the HR department or supervisor or other in-house personnel who aren't up to the task. Assign experienced adjusters instead.

3. **Consider the use of predictive, analytic software which can review data and flag suspicious claims.** Today's high-tech solutions include a variety of predictive and analytic solutions to constantly monitor and alert you to suspicious behavior.

4. **Thoroughly investigate precisely how the injury occurred and gather as much information from the claimant as possible at the time of the incident.** Again, a complete and thorough, up-to-date file in HR will help with this action step.

5. **Immediately contact the employer, the injured claimant, witnesses and medical providers to ask pertinent questions.** Do your due diligence and log all conversations with participating parties.

6. **Record data in such a way that vital contact information that would be given to an outside investigator is readily available.** Any contact information is better than none, and the more information you have on file can help when and if a claimant moves around a lot.

7. **Avoid data entry errors especially with addresses and contact information which can lead to wasted time and money.** Don't let a simple clerical error cost you tens of thousands of dollars when simple preventive maintenance at the earliest of stages, particularly when paperwork is involved, can save you the time, money and hassle.

8. **Establish only one adjuster contact as a foundation for the claim management who initiates communication with all concerned parties.** Too many cooks can spoil the dish, and this is true in workers' comp claims as well as in the kitchen. Having one point of contact, in this case an experienced adjuster, will help you avoid confusion, mixed messages and lost money as a result of inevitable crossed wires that can come from too many people being involved in the investigation.

9. **Direction for further investigation and case management comes from main adjuster contact.** This single contact can help guide

current and future investigatory proceedings in an appropriate and experienced manner.

10. **Hire an experienced investigation firm to take over the role of fact gathering and obtaining the evidence necessary to refute fraudulent compensation claims.** Finally, don't go it on your own. There is a lot of money at risk and in many cases only an experienced investigation firm can properly investigate a seriously fraudulent claim.

The steps of a thorough investigation are clear-cut and well-defined, but only if you follow them to the letter. Be sure that you know both what to investigate, and when, before tackling the investigation on your own.

Case Studies in Claims

To get a feel for the particulars of how these investigations might look, before, during and after, I have provided several case studies my company has performed recently:

Bad Back, Big Plans!

A recent claimant allegedly suffered a back injury while at work for the insured (our client). A tip came in that the claimant was known to be building a house and/or doing construction at an undetermined location. My company was able to capture video surveillance of him actively working on a construction site, lifting several objects and operating a vehicle.

Time to Make the Pizza

Another claimant alleged a head injury after a fall while working for the insured. Surveillance was conducted over a five day period to determine the claimant's activity level.

The claimant was observed to be the only employee working at a pizza shop. In this very active position he was found to be conducting all the business related to the shop including

- Opening the shop
- Putting out signage
- Making pizza
- Interacting with customers
- Earning $$$

As a result of our investigation, a judge rescinded a classification in a recent 114-a decision (i.e. a fraudulent claim) that was based in large part on video surveillance and the testimony of investigator

A Successful Investigative Result!!

A recent claimant had been classified with a marked permanent partial disability for a low back injury. My company provided a DVD with video surveillance of the claimant:

- Climbing a ladder
- Kneeling
- Squatting
- Sitting

- Using a hammer and drill
- Carrying large pieces of metal and...
- WORKING BY HIMSELF ON HIS GARAGE ROOF!

It was determined from our video surveillance that the claimant had only a "mild, residual disability" and that he had "greatly exaggerated his response to light touch during his medical examinations"

The classification was rescinded and the carrier was instructed to suspend payments. A finding was made of zero percent loss of wage earning capacity. The judge commented that the video footage reflected "an individual with significant wage earning capacity and dubious disability."

Another Recent 114-a Decision!

Another recent claimant alleged an injury while working for the insured. Our investigator conducted surveillance on multiple occasions.

During the second surveillance, the subject was observed driving to private residences and plowing their driveways. Due to the damaging surveillance evidence, our investigator was called to testify at the Workers' Compensation Hearing.

Upon conclusion of the hearing, the judge ruled the claimant to be in willful violation of the fraud statute based on material misrepresentations of fact and further ruled that the finding carried a permanent revocation of disability benefits. He even commented on his "Facebook" social media presence! You can read the judge's finding here:

I find the claimant's testimony regarding his work status, his work ability and his operation of a snow plow business in February XXXX incredible. I find that the claimant, when confronted with evidence that he was seeking snow plowing business by his Facebook posts, denied seeking customers and business with explanations that were not believable and not credible. I find that the claimant also misrepresented his work ability... in order to make a claim for temporary total disability awards. I find claimant knowingly made false statements or representation as to material facts for the purpose of influencing a determination regarding his compensation benefits and that the mandatory and discretionary penalties are applicable. Claimant is disqualified from receiving future indemnity benefits in this case after 2/9/xx. No further action is planned by the Board at this time.

The judge's decision was even more damning:

Medical treatment and care, if necessary, for established sites of injury and/or conditions, is authorized. Treatment rendered to one of the body parts covered by the Medical Treatment Guidelines must be consistent with those Guidelines. I find that WCL sec 114-a(1) applies and that the mandatory and discretionary penalties of disqualification from indemnity benefits after February 18, 2014 is warranted.

Clearly, persistent surveillance efforts yield the most fruitful video evidence in assessing an individual's level and capacity for physical activity.

Parting Words

So now you know Investigation 101, which includes when to conduct an investigation and even what to investigate. The "when" can be extremely critical, whether you conduct the investigation yourself or use an agency like ours.

For instance, we recently handled an investigation of a workers' comp claimant who was also an avid hunter. We didn't know this ahead of time, but learned it through social media monitoring.

If we had been given this information earlier we could have done a physical investigation during, say, hunting season to perhaps have caught the claimant on an actual hunt. Again, this story merely reiterates that knowing *what* to investigate is only half the battle – knowing *when* to investigate is equally important.

There is another factor we need to mention, however, so moving forward, in our next chapter we will delve into *who* should conduct the investigation.

CHAPTER 5

Who Should Conduct the Investigation?

Now that we're more familiar with what goes into a workers' comp claim investigation, it's time to consider who should conduct the actual investigation. When it comes to examining the nature of the claims request, there are really only two options:

1. **Hiring an outside agency to conduct the investigation**
2. **Handling the investigation in-house, with your own people**

This chapter will cover the important topic of who should conduct the investigation and, just as importantly, *why*.

Assigning the Investigation

Many insurance carriers and private companies already have a department in place to handle workers' comp claims, fraudulent or otherwise. From risk managers to claims reps, and depending on the size of the HR department, there is typically someone – or several someone's, potentially even a team of someone's in larger companies – who are put in charge of the claim.

Regardless of what the in-house person is actually called, for the purposes of this chapter we'll call him or her the "claims adjuster." And, at some point, the claims adjuster will receive a file that is either fat or thick, depending on when the accident occurred, what type of investigation has been done and how much of a protective plan the company has from before the hire to the employee's first day on the job.

This will become the basis of the claim adjuster's case. He might look through the file, contact a few people, do a few interviews, dig deeper into the claimant's medical files, etc., and come up with a determination around whether or not to pursue an actual investigation.

At this point, the adjuster must decide whether or not he is best suited to pursue an investigation in-house, or if he should hire a third party company to investigate the claim independently.

Many companies opt to handle the investigation, and for a variety of reasons:

- **Financial:** Many companies prefer to conduct their own investigations for simple financial reasons – it's cheaper to handle it in house than hire an investigative firm. They figure they're already going to be paying out, so why go to the extra trouble – and expense – of hiring an investigative firm?
- **Pride:** Some companies want to handle the investigation in-house out of simple pride. They want to keep it "in the family," not share their

dirty laundry with an outside source and handle
the matter internally if at all possible.

- **Simplicity:** For many companies, the simplicity
of simply walking into the break room, taking a
statement from the claimant and calling it a day
is more attractive than hiring an outside firm to
conduct a thorough fraud investigation, even if
it could save them tens of thousands of dollars
in the process.

Whatever the reason a claims adjuster makes for
pursuing the investigation himself, once that choice
is made they typically follow the steps outlined in our
previous chapter.

The Dangers of Mounting an Internal Investigation

While it may save money, time and even face (pride)
in the short-term, in the long-term the decision not to
seek outside help can wind up costing a whole lot more
of all three.

Let's examine a very common case: "Jerry" hurts his
arm on the factory floor, makes an initial claim, consults
a few physicians, makes an even bigger claim and the
case winds up on "Sally," the claim adjuster's desk in
your company.

As per company policy, Sally does an internal
investigation, which can literally be as simple as picking
up the phone and calling Jerry to see what happened.
(I use this example because it happens all the time in
companies both big and small.)

So there Sally is, in her nice comfortable office,
sitting at her desk, staring at a file that could be as

Mario S. Pecoraro

thin as a sheet or two of paper or as thick as a stack of paperwork. Regardless, she picks up the phone and simply calls Jerry.

Jerry answers, hears who it is, answers a few questions, maybe a few questions more, and that's that. Or maybe Jerry is not the claimant. Maybe Sally's being a little more thorough and speaking to any witnesses who might have been there or seen when the accident occurred. Sally asks Jerry some questions, fills in some blanks on her paperwork, ticks off a few boxes and... that's that.

Obviously, this is a very cost- and time-effective way to get "information." Pick up the phone, conduct the interview and write down the facts: date, time, severity, description, name, and address. From a cost and resource perspective, conducting an internal investigation this way makes a lot of sense.

But from an investigatory and cost-saving perspective, your company is at a distinct disadvantage by not at least conducting a face-to-face interview with not only the claimant, but his supervisor(s) and any witnesses.

From an investigative standpoint, body language, eye contact, verbal cues, these all play a major part in determining the truth – or at least the potential for untruth – in an interview subject. Without sitting across from someone, it's extremely difficult to get a sense of their truthfulness. And obviously, who is telling the truth is central to any investigation, let alone a workers' comp claim investigation.

And forget about sitting. One very useful investigation technique is to visit "the scene of the crime," as it were, and have the claimant and/or witnesses simply point to where the accident occurred. This is not only difficult, but impossible to do from your desk and/or during a simple phone investigation.

Face-to-face and on-scene interviews also provide the potential for many more investigative techniques. For instance, Sally can say something to Jerry like, "So, Jerry, can you take me to the site where the accident happened."

"Uh, sure," Jerry can say and, if he walks directly to a certain part of the factory floor, or outside in the maintenance shed or in the field or wherever the accident occurred, speaks with confidence and tells the same story, the same way, half a dozen times, you can be relatively assured of his accuracy. This may lead to larger issues including possible subrogation (recovery) should additional culpability be determined.

If, however, Jerry waffles and is frustrated and seems anxious and his story keeps changing, well... draw your own conclusions. Witnesses are another great source of information, but it's hard to determine if your claims adjuster is sitting behind her desk.

If Sally is out in the field, however, armed with a full array of investigative techniques, she can not only ask direct questions about the incident but indirect ones, such as, "So, Jerry, when the claimant fell off the scaffolding, did you notice any coolers or debris or anything out of the ordinary that might have contributed to the accident?" Or, "Did the claimant seem more agitated or depressed or sleepy at the time of the accident?"

As you can clearly see, there is a world of difference in merely "taking a statement" and conducting a thorough, feet on the ground, face to face investigation. Is it cheaper to sit at a desk and reach for the phone and fill out a form? Absolutely. More expedient? Sure, of course. But is it?

But when tens of thousands of dollars – maybe more – are on the line in the course of an investigation, it can be a lot more effective – time, pride and money wise – in the long run to be more thorough than expedient.

Now, there may be cases where the claim seems simple, straightforward and easily investigated over the phone or through proper channels. But if the claim takes a darker or more expensive turn, if it becomes questionable or red flags begin appearing in even the most basic of answers and/or information, that may be the time to consider an outside investigative agency to protect yourself against possible fraud.

The Team Approach: *A Flaw in the System*

Now, mid-size to larger companies like your own might have an internal investigations or surveillance unit that handles such matters. They may have existing security cameras, security guards, or mystery shoppers, for example. And when a claim is made, a file started, the instinct is to say, "Well, we'll just have our team watch this guy for a couple of days and see what we can come up with."

While on the surface this sounds like a natural, "no brainer" solution to your problem, let's dig a little deeper to uncover a few potential problems with the team approach:

- For one, this is an internal team, conducting an investigation on what amounts to colleagues, coworkers and fellow employees. Their paychecks and the claimant's paycheck are signed by the same employer, creating an instant conflict of interest.

- What's more, you're never quite sure who is investigating who and how close those two are on or off the job. Company picnics and barbecues and team activities tend to bring your employees together, not farther apart, and the possibility of a friend investigating a friend become all the more real in tight-knit companies.

- Finally, internal teams can sometimes feel like the "Internal Affairs" division of an organization and can often be hesitant to come down too hard on fellow employees, for fear of retribution and/ or lack of respect or popularity.

Third party, outside investigative companies share no allegiance to the claimant, his or her colleagues or even the internal claims department. Their job is simply to collect data, gather the facts, conduct a thorough investigation and present the findings, almost clinically, and certainly objectively, to you as the organizational leader.

And even when interior divisions possess state of the art technology or tools to prevent employee theft and fraud, those tools are only as good as the employees operating them.

When to Engage With an Outside Investigator

Case in point: there is a large retailer locally who has their own surveillance van for things like detecting consumer and employee theft, shrinkage and other such routine loss prevention. In the case of an actual claims investigation, they might logically feel like, "Hey, we've got this million dollar van, and all this equipment. Let's go follow this guy around and see if his back really IS messed up."

But having the investigative tools and possessing the experience to use them properly are two different things. Sitting in a surveillance van outside the store watching a customer walk out with a purse full of stolen merchandise isn't the same as tailing a fellow employee around town to see if they're going to the gym, playing golf or boating with their kids when they're supposedly too injured to work.

That kind of detailed surveillance, undercover work and data collection in the field requires a level of expertise beyond most company employees, and therefore often requires an outside source to provide, not to mention the fact that it won't be long before everyone in the company knows the "surveillance van"!

That being said, it's important to determine your own strengths and weaknesses. For instance, if an accident happens on the job and your security cameras capture it, that is absolutely a strength that your internal team can provide over an outside source who wasn't there to capture it at the time.

However, what if the cameras only captured one angle? Or are blurry? Or there is no sound? This is where you can combine a strength that you, your team or your company possess with the additional skill of a third party investigative company to maximize your combined talents to truly arrive at the truth surrounding the existing claim.

There are also training issues that can make the elements of your claim team stronger. For instance, not all claims are fraudulent and not all will require tens of thousands of dollars in payouts. Educating your team on consistency and follow-through can still help you save thousands of dollars in man hours and lost wages by simply helping them assure that injured workers receive the care they need to return to work on time, that they are returning to work on time, that all their paperwork is up to date, etc.

In-house claims departments can be extremely effective, in conjunction with Human Resources and the claimant's supervisor(s) in creating a work environment that embraces both safety and the quickest, safest, healthiest, most effective way to get injured workers back on the job.

Parting Words

Deciding who to run your fraud investigation is never easy, especially when you've worked hard to put an investigative division, team or claims unit in place.

You may feel like putting that division to good use is the reason why you created it in the first place. But detecting actual fraud requires actual experience, and oftentimes only the professionals possess that level of experience to do the job right.

CHAPTER 6

Types of Workers' Comp Investigations

Now that we've explored the multiple facets of how to conduct an investigation, even when to conduct an investigation, I'd like to spend this chapter exploring the multiple different types of workers' comp investigations you might run into. I want this chapter to be a great resource that discusses fraud and the various types of investigations conducted post-incident.

Is the Incident AOE or COE?

Before deciding which type of investigation to pursue, it is critical to determine whether or not the claim originated out of the course of employment or not, often referred to as an Arising Out of Employment (AOE) or a Course of Employment (COE) incident.

In an AOE or COE incident, we are trying to determine if the incident did indeed happen not only on the job but during the course of the employee's regular job duties. It's extremely critical to ascertain if the incident was job related or not, as that carries with it not only a different type of investigation but also various claim categories as well.

Or did the incident occur out of the scope of the workplace, the claimant's assigned duties or even off property. I've seen cases where employees hurt themselves playing soccer or bowling or even doing home repairs over the weekend and came in limping on Monday, hoping no one would notice so they could claim it happened on the job.

Or *did* it happen on the job? Were they where they were supposed to be, doing what they were supposed to do, and thanks to human, mechanical or industrial error, the claimant was injured as he or she said they were? It's important to be objective about each injury and every claim, but to be thorough as well.

That's why the early stages of an investigation are so vitally crucial: to determine what exactly the injury is, how it happened, and where and when it occurred. Emotions are easy but data is hard, and the more data we collect – paperwork, forms, statements, signatures, time stamps and correspondence, the less power emotions and human frailty have to override the cold, hard facts. Human nature is such that witnesses forget crucial evidence, like times and dates, places and faces. Paperwork gets lost, forms don't get filled out, doctors appointments are missed, not logged right or reported, delayed and any variety of other internal and external factors can work to erode the facts so necessary to refuting, or paying out, a claim.

The Scope of an AOE or COE Investigation

So, what goes into investigating an AOE or COE claim? As with any investigation, the goal is to undercover facts, data and, ultimately, the truth. That can be achieved through a variety of means and methods, to include:

- Conducting an initial conference, which we discussed in the previous chapter, with the claims adjuster
- Collecting the claimant's work file, including any and all current assignments
- Doing background research on claimant
- Taking thorough and detailed statements from all witnesses, coworkers, management, supervisors and other pertinent personnel
- Social media searches, keyword searches, screen grabs of pertinent information
- Documenting all new and ongoing interactions with claimant
- Reviewing the extent of the workers' comp file, if any
- Continually updating the claim file with new information, updates, interviews, documents, medical records, files

As you can see, thoroughness is the letter of the day and the more facts and data you provide before, during and after the injury, the better your chances of disputing or mitigating the losses that often arise with such a claim.

Subrogation: *Who's to Blame?*

One issue that often comes up with a workers' compensation claim is that of subrogation or, as Google. com defines it, "the substitution of one person or group by another in respect of a debt or insurance claim, accompanied by the transfer of any associated rights and duties."

In layman's terms, subrogation is simply the spreading out of blame, risk and cost among various parties. For instance, let's say you've got a construction worker out on a job and he falls off a piece of scaffolding, severely injuring his leg.

During the course of the workers' comp investigation, you discover that the manufacturer of the scaffolding was at fault for using shoddy equipment, or the contractor outsourced by the scaffolding company didn't assemble it properly, or it was damaged in transit by the transportation or delivery company.

Suddenly you're looking at a variety of subrogation opportunities, in which the scaffolding company, the contractor who put it together, the delivery company or the vendor can, should and possibly will share in the blame or, if the investigation determines as such, shoulder the majority of the payout.

Subrogation claims are quite common and, once you've determined that the injury was work-related – i.e. AOE or COE – the next step would be to determine if your company is entirely to blame or if there were other, mitigating and subrogating circumstances that might spread the responsibility around and thus lessen the financial penalty to your organization.

In legitimate and real world costs, consider your injured construction worker who may be permanently disabled. Without investigating third party error, negligence or culpability, you – and your insurance carrier – might be shouldering the entire burden of his long-term care and compensation. But if a thorough investigation reveals additional parties were at fault, they might be responsible for seventy percent or more of the burden, thus relieving you of the lion's share of the financial responsibility. Thus it is critical that you consider all areas of culpability related to the injury, and not just your own.

The aspects of a subrogation investigation might include the following:

- Digging deeper to discover all parties involved in the accident
- Once obtained, determining which insurance carriers cover all involved parties
- Signed release forms from all medical personnel and outside interviews and witness statements
- Curating all documentation and contact information for insurance carriers, contractors, vendors, and employees related to the claim
- Securing all court, medical and insurance records
- Keeping accurate records of all communication with related carriers

Subrogation investigations should be thorough, detailed and far-reaching. While every item on the list above is critical to an investigation's success, some cry out for further discussion. For instance, when it comes to getting signed release forms for medical records, this is an extremely important step to lock down. After all, medical records are key to any claim investigation, and not just those related to the incident. Consider a claim where a worker might be complaining of back pain, shoulder or joint pain, knee pain, etc.

Securing releases to examine previous medical records, examinations, x-rays and other tests might reveal that, a month prior to the incident in question, he was in the same doctor's office already complaining of knee pain from a waterskiing accident, or a torn ligament from a bowling injury. Without those signed release forms and valuable medical records, particularly previous to the incident, this information might not have otherwise come to light.

Despite the work involved, conducting a thorough subrogation investigation can be well worth the time and effort if it is indeed discovered that a third – or even fourth or fifth parties – can help share the financial burden of an expensive workers' comp claim.

The Sub-Rosa Investigation

If it is determined that fraud is, or even if it may be in play, a sub rosa investigation – which is another word for subrogation should be initiated.

While all investigations should be thorough, this is naturally a more thorough, prolonged and active investigation to clear the company of all wrongdoing and liability and shift the blame to the claimant.

This type of investigation might include the following:

- Complete background research into the claimant, including all off-duty and extracurricular activities
- A thorough online and social media investigation
- Video, audio and photographic evidence taken while doing surveillance
- Verbal and written reports before, during and after each instance of surveillance

- Transcribing and attaching all verbal, audio and video surveillance to attach with audio and visual files
- Complete and absolute compliance with all local, state and federal rules and regulations concerning the scope of your investigation.

Regardless of whether or not you are conducting the sub rosa investigation yourself, or outsourcing it to an investigative agency, ensure that you or your investigators understand their responsibility to testify in various courts, appeals, arbitrations and in depositions.

This is where investigation becomes more active rather than passive, and fieldwork comes more and more into play with items like surveillance, documentation, pursuit and observation.

As technology becomes more advanced and fraudulent activity more sophisticated, it is important to be proactive in keeping up to date with surveillance tools and activities. For instance, we're currently experimenting with using drones and other remote recording devices for surveillance, in addition to our regular methods of stationary and mobile surveillance vehicles.

Preparing for an Investigation

Regardless of the type of investigation you will be conducting, preparation begins by quickly ramping up to speed on all the applicable data that has already been archived, in relation to what else might be needed to conduct a thorough investigation pursuant to the claim.

One of the top priorities when conducting any claims investigation is to dig deep into the types of coverage the carrier provides and what it means for your organization, in dollars and cents.

Knowing what you are and aren't liable for is key to estimating damages, and integral to helping the investigator know what to look for to avoid claims of liability.

Knowing the paragraphs and clauses of the coverage generally begins with obtaining the actual insurance contract that will apply to the claimant in question. Since insurance policies can often be akin to legalese, it is important to parse the policy through an investigator or adjustor who is experienced with such policies and can thus "translate" them for you and your leadership team.

In addition to paperwork like insurance, preparation would include opening the pathways of communication with critical liaisons at key pressure points of the investigation, to include the insurance company, any medical offices that might be integral to the investigation, as well as key leadership, supervisory, management and coworker spokespeople.

Securing Information: *Statements*

Information is at the heart of every claims investigation, and as we proceed through the process of instigating a claim we will begin with one of the first and foremost aspects of any investigation: securing statements.

Statements come in many forms:

- Injury statements
- Personal statements
- Witness statements

- Medical statements
- Financial statements

Here we begin with collecting, as soon as possible, personal statements from the claimant as well as witness statements from anyone in the vicinity at the time of the incident in question.

Obtaining statements will include the full cooperation of the claimant's supervisors and leadership team, so it is important that critical staff know that an investigation is ongoing and to cooperate fully with that investigation.

I can't tell you how many times my team and I experience "push back" from employees we're trying to obtain statements from, even though we're essentially "on their side" trying to save their company tens of thousands of dollars in insurance claims.

The first statement, of course, should come from the injured person – as soon as possible – and should include:

- What happened before, during and after the injury, to the best of his/her knowledge
- Day, time and shift of the accident, as closely as possible
- Names and contact information of any witnesses to the injury
- Any medical attention, on or off site, he or she may have received pursuant to the injury and contact information of healthcare provider(s)

Naturally, the sooner this statement – and the resulting information – is obtained, the better. From this statement, typically, comes a ripple effect of additional statements that need to be taken, from witnesses, supervisors, medical and healthcare staff.

In addition to personal and witness statements, additional statements will include paperwork, files, financial statements and other supporting evidence to either help prove or disprove the injured employee's claim.

As statements, paperwork and evidence come in, they should be carefully analyzed for signs of fault, liability and even fraud. In other words:

- Was the employee responsible? The employer?
- Was faulty equipment or another contractor/ subcontractor to blame?
- Were alcohol or drugs involved?
- Was the injury self-inflicted?
- Was the injury suffered on or off the job?

Investigations can be complicated and no set outcome should be assumed before, during or even after the data becomes pouring in. For instance, a delivery driver may have had alcohol in his or her system at the time of an accident and/or injury, but that doesn't mean they're entirely at fault if, say, the vehicle had faulty brakes, used tires or wasn't properly maintained.

In addition, the stretch of road and its condition may be partly at fault, as might be discovered when the investigation reveals a dozen or more similar incidents in the same vicinity. Keep an open mind and be objective during the investigation, letting the statement's evidence tell the story instead of using them to support the story you feel is the "right" one.

Investigations In the Case of Litigation

If it is ultimately determined that a case will be litigated in court, through appeals or arbitration, the investigation naturally takes on a different caliber, energy level and tone of sophistication.

The claimant's file should be brought up to date as quickly, and as thoroughly, as possible, to include:

- Obtaining any missing documents
- Securing any statements that haven't been recorded or transcribed
- Filing, scanning, copying or obtaining paperwork to ensure the file is complete
- Transcribing any and all audio and video evidence

I can't stress enough how important it is to treat every investigation as if it might go to court, with the same urgency and attention to detail. In particular, personal, supervisory and witness statements need to be obtained as quickly as possible before memories fade, times get confused or facts muddled.

Every statement that is nailed down early pins the giver of the statement to his or her words, which then become more difficult to dispute if they change their minds – or perhaps become sympathetic to the claimant – over the course of the investigation.

Having best practices in place, as we've discussed in the earlier chapters of this book, will help ensure that this work is done properly, done quickly and, above all, done thoroughly to ensure that facts take precedence over emotion if the case should come to litigation.

Preparing Statements for Litigation

If you think of statements as evidence, as proof, then you are likely to view them in the spirit in which they are intended. Whenever you take a statement from an individual – be it the claimant, his or her coworkers, management, friends, family, medical or healthcare personnel – it is a signed and sworn document that purports to tell the truth.

Those sworn statements are critical pieces of evidence, no different than medical tests, lab reports and the like, that either serve to prove the claimant's story or disprove it. The more timely, more accurate and more specific these statements are, the better your evidence in court.

Statements can be taken verbally, video-recorded or written up, but in my experience all statements should be professionally transcribed to ensure that they are more readily absorbed and understood by all interested parties. Keep all files, but use the transcribed statements in day-to-day proceedings.

Also, when it comes to statements, always err on the side of caution. If there were twelve witnesses to the incident and you only interviewed eleven of them, who's to say that the twelfth statement won't be the one that exonerates – or at least mitigates – your culpability in the incident? Why not take it?

Who should you take statements from? In addition to the injured party, you may want to take statements from:

- Witnesses
- Medical and healthcare personnel at/on the scene

- The claimant's dependents or nearest relatives
- Coworkers, colleagues and supervisors

When considering who to interview, ask yourself who would know the claimant best? In terms of fraudulent claims, who might be a party – or witness – to the claimant's activities? Perhaps a spouse or child can tell you how active the claimant was, or is, or has been. A teammate or league member might inform you about the claimant's physical state or current standings in the organization. In other words, consider who might know the claimant best and be able to shed light, truthfully, on his or her present condition.

Also remember that statements are not isolated documents, nor do they exist in a vacuum. From each statement should come kernels, or nuggets, of information – clues – that might lead to potential surveillance points or stakeouts.

For instance, interviewing a claimant's spouse might reveal that, yes, they are injured and act injured, but weren't always. When pressed for their old hangouts, the spouse might reveal the claimant was active in the local VFW chapter and bowling league, which now provides you with two potential outlets to surveil in your ongoing investigation.

Preparing the Investigative Report

Finally, the investigative report should be prepared to ensure that it is easily and quickly absorbed by all interested parties, including both teams of lawyers, the judiciary, witnesses, legal aids, etc.

The report may or may not use captions, depending on who is requesting it and/or their preferences. Ideally, you should prepare a professional, clean, easy to understand and digest report, and use it as a template for further summaries.

Whoever is running the investigation may be required to relate an opinion as to the guilt or innocence of the claimant. In such cases, do so professionally, not personally, and remember to rely on data, not emotion, in your summary.

Remember, too, that this report is intended to summarize the case as a whole, while not containing the entire case. "Highlighting" specific statements, pertinent information and evidence will guide those in authority where to look for the entire document, file, recording or transcript.

As to contents, the following line items should be a good guide as to what to include in your investigative report:

- The Insured
- Insurance Coverage Data (if permitted)
- The Claimant (if not represented by counsel)
- Dependents (in fatal or potential death cases)
- Wage Information
- Injuries
- Medical Data (where permitted)
- Facts of Accident or Exposure
- Witnesses/Supervisor of the Claimant
- Subrogation
- Safety
- Discussion of Miscellaneous Factors Peculiar to the Case
- Outline of Unfinished Investigation
- Recommendations of Investigator

Again, different departments may want different formats for your investigative report, but the above information will generally be required regardless of the format it's eventually compiled with.

Parting Words: *A Word About Premium Fraud*

One type of investigation that exists but doesn't necessarily fall under the claimant's territory is that of "premium fraud." In other words, a company misrepresents his or her function, industry or level of involvement in a particular category in order to lower his annual workers' comp insurance premiums.

We all know that workers' comp insurance isn't cheap, but it's required and the right way to lower premiums is to simply be diligent in preventing injury in the first place.

What some companies do, however, is misrepresent – intentionally or "accidentally," a little or a lot – the kinds of premiums they should be paying. For instance, a construction company might have eighty employees on payroll. Each "type" of employee is classified in a particular category of premium payment, based on risk of injury, known danger of the job, hazards of employment, etc.

Let's say the company has seventy construction workers and ten office workers, but "misrepresents" that figure. They claim ten construction workers and seventy office employees. On paper, it might not stand out and, in fact, the owner of the company could go for years, even decades, paying a far lower premium than if he had accurately claimed his office to construction worker split.

In case of an injury, however, if a claim is made the "oversight" or misrepresentation comes to light, causing the insurance company to retroactively pursue the rightful amount they should have been paid all those years, sometimes to the tune of hundreds of thousands of dollars. I've literally seen companies go out of business trying to pay their back premiums, and owners who regretted engaging in what basically amounts to premium fraud for all those years.

CHAPTER 7

The Secrets of Surveillance

Surveillance is a critical factor in determining fraud; either proving it, or disproving it. Now more than ever, surveillance is a crucial step in both preventing and ascertaining fraud, as fraud itself is reaching near epidemic proportions.

According to the *Insurance Fraud Handbook* put together by the Association of Certified Fraud Examiners, "One of the most pressing issues facing modern day insurance carriers is the identification and investigation of fraud. With estimates ranging from $80 billion to $110 billion a year, insurance fraud is a growing concern within the industry. Current estimates show that 10 cents of every dollar earned is lost due to fraud."

This chapter will focus on what I call the "secrets" of surveillance. These will encompass such items as how to gather intelligence, privacy issues, the plaintiff's point of view and even the legal aspects of how much is too much when it comes to conducting surveillance.

First, let's shape our discussion around the topic of surveillance by agreeing on a firm definition of the term itself. According to *Privacy, Surveillance and the Law: Guidelines for Investigators & Claims Examiners* by noted industry experts Larry G. Henning and Edward J. Wilbraham, surveillance can be defined thusly: "In the context of insurance investigations, covert surveillance is the observation of an individual from a hidden or unknown position to document the extent of a subject's physical activities."

Now that we agree on what surveillance is, let's determine how to conduct it.

Gathering Intelligence

Intelligence – or the obtaining of facts, evidence and testimony to prove or disprove fraud – is the meat and muscle of any fraud investigation. When it comes to surveillance, it is what you're actually looking for while on surveillance.

Gathering intelligence begins with the subject: himself, or herself.

Where Does the Subject Live?

We want to know the physical address, sure, but there are also a variety of other factors to consider, including:

- **Does the subject have a metropolitan address, with city streets, multiple levels, and a parking garage?** City investigations naturally provide a different level of complexity, nuance and investigation than an investigation being conducted elsewhere.
- **Or does he/she have a rural address where the nearest neighbor lives three miles away?** Rural investigations provide their own complications and challenges as well.

All of these naturally have implications for gathering intelligence through active surveillance. For instance, where do you park outside a downtown Manhattan highrise with 400 units and a private parking garage? These and a variety of other factors all have to be taken into account when conducting a thorough surveillance.

Learning and Logistics

There are many logistics to account for and plans to make. For instance, if a subject's residence has three ways of getting to and from the main road, how many surveillance teams will you need to fully investigate him? Can a single team watch one main point of entry and exact with video on the other two? Or will you need three active teams? All of these factors contribute to both the complexity and cost of an investigation.

Other Factors to Consider

There are a variety of other factors to consider before conducting a surveillance investigation as well, not the least of which is who from within the investigative firm is the best fit? In other words:

- **Will a female investigator blend in more than a male investigator?** Perhaps you need someone to follow the subject into areas where it makes the most sense to send in a female investigator, such as a women's only gym.
- **Do you need someone who speaks a particular language to interact reasonably with neighbors, colleagues and the like?** In areas

where you have a largely Hispanic, Korean or other language being spoken, you will want to send an investigator who not only speaks – and understands – the language but blend in with the surrounding culture as well.

- **Will a middle-aged white investigator stand out too prominently in the subject's neighborhood and favorite hangouts?** Perhaps your subject is young and his pursuits are dominantly youthful, like working out or going to nightclubs or hanging out in areas where an older, more sedentary investigator might attract attention.

- **Or will you need an investigator of a certain age, race or ethnicity to blend in better?** Again, you will want your investigators to "blend into the background" as much as possible to avoid suspicion.

- **Is it a dangerous area known to have criminal or drug activity?** The more dangerous, challenging or complicated a subject's home and hangouts are, the more experienced an investigator or team you will need to gather intelligence on him or her.

- **Is it in a rural area where the neighbors all know each other and will spot an "outsider" immediately?** Such investigations naturally pose an additional layer of challenge and complexity as well.

There is no "one size fits all" investigation. Knowing the lay of the land means all the various factors that may creep up and surprise you later will help when planning a thorough surveillance investigation.

Knowing the various factors that surround each particular subject will help your investigators plan carefully, and fully, before budgeting too few hours to elicit the intelligence you need to fight your case.

What I see quite often, however, are companies assigning out too little in terms of resources – not enough manpower, resources or hours – to conduct a thorough enough investigation based on all the parameters involved.

It can often require significant costs to conduct a thorough investigation, but weight them against the satisfaction – and savings – of thoroughly fighting an active fraud investigation before you decide to scrimp on surveillance.

Legal Issues

While you don't need a law degree to fight against insurance fraud, no chapter on conducting surveillance would be complete without at least addressing the variety of legal issues that arise when gathering intelligence in today's modern, litigious climate.

According to *Privacy, Surveillance and the Law: Guidelines for Investigators & Claims Examiners* by noted industry experts Larry G. Henning and Edward J. Wilbraham, "Most litigation involving improper surveillance procedures or techniques is based upon legal theories of trespass, invasion of privacy, unfair claims practice, defamation, slander, bad faith, and intentional infliction of emotional distress." So it's important to ensure that you know your own current state law – or that your investigator does – regarding surveillance.

That said, the general question concerning legality often comes down to the insured's right to privacy versus the insurer's right to investigate. In other words, what rights can the subject of your investigation expect to enjoy versus how free are you to investigate him?

While policies, regulations and laws vary from city to city and state to state (see note at the end of this section), there are some basic guidelines for investigators to follow when conducting surveillance.

Backyards and Exteriors

Obviously, you can't trespass on private property, even if it's on behalf of an active surveillance. However, let's say your subject's backyard sits at a lower elevation than the public street that's behind it, and is clearly visible from plain view. Then the subject's reasonable expectation of privacy is minimized because of that location. If you can see something from public view, it's well within the domain of an active surveillance.

Windows

Again, trespassing is restricted but does the subject keep his or her windows open? Are his or her activities clearly visible, through the windows, from the public and/or street view? If so, then his activities are fair game.

I once had a case where a claimant claimed he was totally disabled, to the point where he had to drag himself up the stairs in his house while sitting on his rear end. While he had most of his windows covered, we observed that one window revealed his staircase and during active surveillance we could see him clearly walking up the stairs just fine.

Of course, like I said earlier, every district, state, city, court and judge are different, so you have to be as careful as possible but knowing the law will help you avoid the intelligence being thrown out.

Pretext Use

One question that always tends to arise during an active surveillance investigation is the legality of using a pretext during your investigation. A pretext is simply using a ruse or false "pretext" for obtaining intelligence during an investigation.

A pretext might range from holding an empty dog leash in your hand while knocking on the subject's door and pretending to be looking for your lost pet or calling the subject's house inquiring about a "long, lost Uncle Fred."

Whatever pretext you use might involve repercussions, ethical, professional, legal or otherwise. Particularly if a subject is represented – i.e. represented by an attorney – you're prevented from making a direct approach without seeking counsel's permission or even attendance first.

However, you can still make a direct approach – using a pretext, ruse or otherwise – for that subject's family, friends, coworkers, neighbors, bowling team members, drinking buddies, etc.

Just like you need to pre-strategize where a subject lives before planning or conducting a surveillance, consider whether or not a pretext will even work considering the subject's circumstances.

If it's a very tight-knit, rural community where everybody knows everybody, walking up to the nearest neighbor – who may live four or five miles away from the subject – with an empty dog leash isn't going to be quite as effective a pretext as it might be in a more concentrated, city-type investigation.

Privacy

How much privacy can a subject expect? We've touched on this before, but particularly when it comes to surveillance, as a general rule the farther away from the subject's property he or she is, the less privacy he can expect. Again, you will want to consult with local legalities as well as the insurance company with prior approval to ensure that what you're doing is both ethically and legally sound. There are a variety of ways to observe a subject in public places without invading his or her privacy, to include:

- Gyms and sports clubs
- Restaurants and nightclubs
- VFW/Other membership posts
- Places of worship

As always, check with local city and state as well as national policies – or insist that your investigator does – to ensure that your surveillance, testimony and intelligence won't be unduly challenged because you crossed the line during your investigation.

Consider the Plaintiff's Point of View

It may help investigators and employers to understand what the plaintiff – i.e. your subject – knows about investigation policies and practices in order to be more effective while conducting surveillance.

No doubt, their legal counsel will "coach" them to the realities of a possible investigation. I have seen cases where a plaintiff's attorney literally coaches them in the lobby of the hearing that an investigator will be watching while we were listening to the conversation!

They will very likely school them in all your methods of investigation which will them make your job as an investigator – or a company hiring an investigator – even more difficult.

They will coach them on other aspects as well, such as:

- How to avoid posting personal pictures, videos or even comments on social media
- Avoiding displays of physical activity during the investigation
- Staying indoors to ensure privacy during an active investigation
- What needs to be turned over to the other (i.e. "your") side in the legal discovery process

Whatever your subject's counsel may have told them or not, always assume that your subject knows you're investigating them and act accordingly.

Also, work from a position of power. Be smarter, wiser and know the law. For instance, when it comes to discovery, counsel only has to alert the plaintiff's counsel that there is, say, video evidence to be used against the subject. You don't have to say how much, or what the video is of, or even how long the video is. It might be ten minutes, ten hours or ten days of surveillance video, but that doesn't have to be disclosed in discovery.

Use such legal loopholes to your advantage by collecting as much surveillance data and intelligence as possible to make it appear your case is possibly much stronger than it is. Some fraudulent subjects will naturally assume they've been found out and act accordingly as well.

Common Surveillance Tools, Tactics and Techniques

The following "laundry list" includes some of today's most common surveillance tools, tactics and techniques:

- You will naturally want to actively monitor and maintain surveillance around the subject's location and residence.
- You will want to actively monitor any and all of the subject's social media accounts for intelligence, as well as their coworkers, friends and family.
- Neighbors, family and friends are always vital in conducting a surveillance investigation. Using pretexts to interview neighbors, family members and in particular girl and boyfriends can pay off in spades for the determined investigator.
- Another aspect of the surveillance that needs to be highlighted here is the subject's independent medical examination, or IME. What we commonly do is actively investigate the subject the day before the IME, the day of

the IME and then again on the day after the IME. That's because investigation savvy subjects might "behave" on the day of their actual IME, knowing they'll most likely be under surveillance, but then likely misbehave the day before or after the independent medical examination because, after all, who would/could be watching them then?

These strategies have proven effective in the past, and are likely to succeed in the future, because they rely on the fraudulent subject's inability to behave as he or she regularly might, even though they are claiming to be incapacitated.

Miscellaneous Tools

There are a variety of modern tools the investigator can use to further his or her surveillance of an unwitting subject, including:

- **Remote cameras with sensors.** These are commonly used in hunting scenarios and are excellent and easy to conceal.
- **Remote devices.** Many modern tools rely on utilizing remote technology to increase visibility while still respecting a subject's right to privacy.
- **Remote vehicles.** This is one of the simplest methods of leaving a vehicle in an area the subject is known to frequent, either with a camera running or a motion sensitive camera that works when movement is present.

- **Covert Cameras.** State-of-the-art covert cameras have really helped take investigations to a whole other level. Case in point: we have key fob cameras where we can walk into a restaurant or lounge, set our "keys" on the bar, counter or table top and secretly record the subject in a variety of public settings without their knowledge.

Technology is such that this list keeps growing with each passing day and, likely by the time of this book's publication, several new surveillance tools, tactics and techniques will have emerged. Make sure that either you or your investigator stays abreast of the latest and greatest of them.

Parting Words: *Best Practices for Amount of Surveillance*

Finally, have and follow various best practices when it comes to the amount of surveillance you intend to conduct. How much is too much, not enough or just enough? From my point of view, always conduct at least eight to twelve hours of surveillance to start on any assignment, and never less. Why?

At the going rate, when you factor in manpower, tools, technology, scope and planning, it costs nearly as much to conduct an eight, ten or twelve-hour investigation as it does a six-hour, four-hour or less investigation. Why go to all the trouble and spend less time investigating when it costs roughly the same?

It's also important to stay abreast of the amount of time spent on the investigation, what's transpired, and what you would still like to see happen. Knowing what intelligence you're gathering, the complexities – and effectiveness – of the surveillance can help you seek recommendations to continue or discontinue based upon results thus far. Finally, it's important to gain actionable intelligence – information that results in answers, not questions, solutions, not problems – before deciding whether to continue with, or abort, the investigation.

Staying abreast of the time, energy, manpower and resources you're devoting to the surveillance can be useful when determining how effective it is, and whether or not it will ultimately be useful in defending a fraudulent workers' comp claim.

CHAPTER 8

What to Expect During an Investigation

When it's determined that you need the services of an investigative agency, or you're using your own team, to conduct a workers' comp claim investigation, it's important to know what to expect. Plan for costs and time involved, as well as how many hours will be spent per day, how many teams are needed per day, and how many people are needed for each team.

These are all questions that beg to be answered, and the sooner the better.

Six Steps for Setting the Expectations in Advance

One way to ensure that you know, up front, what to expect from the investigation and the company (team) providing it is to follow Six Steps for Setting the Expectations in Advance:

Step 1: *Budget*

First, consider your budget for the investigation: how much you have to spend, how much you want to spend, and what you can get for the money involved.

Like any significant expense of time, energy, resources and money, you want to see a solid return on your investment. But just like in real estate, don't "over build" an investigation if it's going to cost more than what an eventual payout would.

One thing we like to remind clients is to compare the size of the claim and/or the risk of financial exposure – low risk, medium risk, high risk, etc. – when considering the budget for the investigation.

If it's a low risk case, budget accordingly. Do your due diligence, but not to the point where you're spending millions of dollars on it. Same with medium risk cases or high. That said, you don't want to skimp on any investigation. If you do a shoddy investigation, or don't have enough in the budget to gather all the information you need, it's going to show and, if that's the case, why bother doing an investigation at all. From my experience, a surveillance should always consist of at least twenty four (24) hours, conducted in four (4) hour increments, over the course of several days in order to attempt to establish a pattern. Anything less will generally result in little or no value to all parties.

Step 2: *Determine the Investigation Type*

Once you set the scope of your budget, it's important to determine the type of the investigation you're paying for. Many clients think by saying, "go investigate" a firm knows what they're talking about, but there are levels of investigation to consider, particularly in today's modern world. In general, the most common types of investigation we see today are either social media or surveillance, or combinations of both. But we won't know which if we don't ask.

So be upfront to determine such issues as:

- Is this a social media investigation?
- Is the social media investigation ongoing, meaning at intervals throughout the day, week or even month (if budgeted for)?
- Or is it a one-time query into a day's online events?
- Is it a surveillance investigation?
- How intense is the surveillance intended to be?
- Or is it a combination of social media and surveillance?

The sooner you know the specific type of investigation you want to conduct, the sooner the investigative firm can begin to use the budget you've allotted and plan accordingly.

Step 3: *Set Specific Requirements*

Every investigation is unique and so is every client. It's important that both parties understand, right away, what the specific requirements of the investigation are going to look like. For instance:

- How often does the client want updates?
- Are they to be verbal, such as on a conference or Skype call?
- Or written updates, via email, text, snail mail, etc.?
- Verbal and written updates?
- Who needs to be communicated with, exactly?

- Who is the preferred contact and what is his/her number?

The longer an investigation continues, and the more working parts it entails – teams, size of teams, vehicles, and number of vehicles – the more important these specific requirements become.

Step 4: *Unique Requirements*

Some clients have extenuating circumstances that require, in addition to the usual specific requirements mentioned in Step 3, more unique requirements. For instance:

- **Is it a rural case that will require an added layer and level of surveillance?** Rural cases involve a more sophisticated approach by means of simple geography and the "stranger danger" that comes from folks in rural areas knowing who tends to come and go from nearby properties.
- **Does the client prefer covert cameras as opposed to live surveillance?** There are different layers of complexity and cost between both methods of surveillance that need to be taken into account.
- **Are the investigators allowed to use pretexts, such as pretending to be a survey taker or looking for a lost dog?** We have some clients who are absolutely against pretexting, which tends to tie our hands a bit when it comes to gathering intelligence from family, friends, neighbors and coworkers.

- **Are there individuals the investigation should not record or follow?** For instance, such as a young child, spouse or other relative? Some clients tell us, "If the claimant is seen with his young children, stop recording right away." The sooner we know that, the sooner we can respond by complying with the client's wishes.
- **Does the client have equipment of their own?** Some clients have recording equipment or remote equipment that might aid in the investigation and cut down on cost if we decide to use it.
- **Is it an environment where the client needs to employ a certain race or gender of investigator?** For instance, we had a case recently where a male investigator, under a pretext, was visiting a Muslim home where the women weren't allowed to open the door to a male without a male being home. We had to send a female out instead, a costly and time-consuming mistake that could have been avoided if we had known about the claimant's religious beliefs in advance.

Obviously, the sooner an investigative firm knows these unique requirements, the sooner they can budget, allot and account for them before conducting the actual investigation.

Step 5: *Spell it Out*

As with any service, field investigators aren't mind readers. Spell out your needs very specifically. Whatever you do, do not ASSUME the investigator can you read your mind; let the firm know what you are seeking, hopefully in writing, from the very outset so that everyone is on the same page.

If you're looking to find out if a subject is injured or not, say so. But don't stop there: discuss the nature of the injuries, what specific fraud you might suspect, and what your ideal results might be.

For instance, a very specific, detailed request might sound something like: "Our subject claims to have hurt his arm to the degree that he can no longer use it for work or even recreation purposes. However, we have heard that he is still in a bowling league and fishes regularly. If we could verify those claims, or disprove them, we would consider this a successful investigation."

There is no reason to withhold information from the investigative agency, whether consciously or subconsciously. Simply lay out the case from start to finish and express your needs so that the firm can respond to them in a timely manner.

Step 6: *Be Realistic*

Finally, understand that conducting an investigation is not a guarantee of finding contradictory behavior. That's why it's called an investigation. Not every surveillance will deliver adverse results. In fact, many don't, however it does help to assess the liability and exposure on a claim.

However, a reasonable and effective amount of surveillance will maximize your chances of finding out the truth relative to your suspected fraudulent claims. The key is to set the stage for a successful investigation by following the above Six Steps for Setting the Expectations in Advance.

Keep the Lines of Communication Open

Another way to insure a successful investigation is to start with an open line of communication and keep it open throughout the course of the investigation. Begin with a simple confirmation with your contact person that outlines the following:

- Acknowledging receipt of the assignment
- How long the assignment is expected to take
- When it will begin
- Specific benchmark dates and times, such as the beginning, middle and end of the investigation
- The investigator or investigators assigned to the case and relevant contact information
- The case manager and his or her contact information and office hours

In addition to who is conducting the investigation and how long it might take or cost, honest and open communication about the scope of the investigation is critical to the case's success. For instance:

- **Social media:** What types of social media should be investigated, how often, and how varied
- **Vehicles:** How many vehicles should be followed, and which types
- **Area:** Is the area to be investigated rural, city, any special requirements for surveillance of area
- **Statements, if applicable:** Will the client require written statements from various witnesses and, if so, which ones?

Knowing what is, and isn't, covered in an investigation helps you, as the client, to manage expectations and the investigative firm to provide the right kind of data to assist in the case.

Give Regular Updates

Also when it comes to communication, it's important that the investigative firm gives regular updates to the client to ensure they're being made aware of any relevant data, or even if there is data to report. Sometimes there won't be, frankly.

One fairly obvious point of communication would be to confirm that the claimant the investigative firm is following is the subject in question. In other words, when surveillance is requested, the client should include a facial/positive ID shot early on in the investigation. In fact, one of the first updates should be to send the client video or photographic evidence to ensure you're investigating the right person!

If it's a non-surveillance case, such as going out and taking witness statements, the client should be informed, on a regular basis, how those efforts are progressing. If the witness is being unresponsive, has been called in several times to make a statement and hasn't shown, the investigative firm should be honest with the client and report that no progress has been made, rather than waiting weeks or months to reveal the same information.

The same goes for specific requests the client has made. The investigative firm should do their investigative due diligence and report the findings, for better or worse. They should have systematic, regular and routine ways of doing this, for every client and every investigation, every time. The investigative firm should make it very clear for the client what is being done, by whom, when and where, and what result was determined.

Even if the firm is not getting the results the client might be seeking, at least they're conducting the investigation to the best of their abilities and letting the client know the specifics of who, what, when, where and why. Open lines of communication make it clear not only what the client expects, but what the investigative firm is willing to do to meet those expectations.

For instance, if during the course of surveillance the investigative firm finds two witnesses who were reportedly at the scene when the claimant fell, it's imperative that they not only investigate those two witnesses but inform the client about them and update regularly as to their discoveries concerning said witnesses.

Be clear on how regularly you want updates. Typically our clients want updates after every eight-hour cycle of surveillance, at which point we prepare a simple report and pass it along to the appropriate contact person(s).

Once that confirmation is made, and you have communicated this to the investigative firm, have them proceed with the investigation. For non-surveillance, such as taking statements or gathering information, the investigative firm should know what additional steps need to be taken based upon the direction of the investigation.

Be specific about how you want to be communicated with and what types of updates you want. For instance, many clients want both verbal and written updates, and it's always good to have everything pertaining to an investigation in writing.

Increasingly, clients are expecting us to provide whatever videos and photographic evidence we've obtained in all updates, whenever possible! Fortunately, technology makes this easier than ever.

As these updates and communications begin to pile up, the client should determine whether case continues after/above the amount of initial hours authorized or if it's time to request a final report and call the investigation quits.

At this point, if the case continues, the investigative firm should continue to follow same process as before. In other words, open communication helps the client dictate whether or not to continue the investigation at the same rate, a reduced rate or possibly an increased rate.

It's really up to them, not only to approve the continuing investigation but communicate that to the investigative firm as well. If the case does not continue and all the investigative hours have been exhausted, then a final report should be prepared and sent.

When and how soon? Typically we like to prepare and send a final report within five to seven days of our last update to the client. Many clients expect immediate results. However, reproducing video surveillance and scanning all photographic evidence, as well as proofing field reports and assembling all collateral data can take close to – or more than – a week depending on the length and degree of sophistication of the investigation.

Submitting the Final Report

When it comes time to submitting the final report and invoice, clarity is key. For accuracy and timeliness, our agency lists the following when submitting a final report:

- **Background and Injury:** What was the nature of the accident? Where and when did it occur? What was the nature of the actual injury? Severity?
- **Aerial/photo/layout (if applicable) of the area:** We provide photos or geographical map findings of the areas of surveillance, if necessary. This can include, for example, photos/representations of the claimant's home, workplace, favorite haunts, or where specifically relevant findings were made.
- **Summary of Findings:** For surveillance and non-surveillance cases alike, we then provide a "summary of findings," identifying the claimant, the claim number, the insured party, the specific request, the specific dates of service and whether or not the claimant was observed:

Claimant:	LAST NAME, First
Your Claim#:	99999999
Insured:	ABC Manufacturing
Request:	Surveillance
Dates of Service:	8/7/15, 8/8/15, 8/15/15
Claimant Observed:	Yes

- **Written depiction of summary:** In addition to the visual summary, we provide an extensive, even exhaustive, written summary of what steps were taken and what information resulted from each surveillance, interview, witness statement and observation. Rather than merely presenting a lump paragraph or two, the summary should be broken down clearly with subheadings such as: INTERVIEW, CLAIMANT BACKGROUND, NORMAL DAILY ACTIVITIES, CLAIMANT HOBBIES, FAMILY HISTORY, PRIOR WORK HISTORY, etc. Under each subheading would be a succinct description of what we found. For instance, "Claimant John Doe was interviewed about his various hobbies and expressed an interest in baseball collecting and bowling. Stated that, since the injury, he has not been able to bowl."

- **Video surveillance:** Whatever video was recorded should be copied and uploaded to a secure site for the client's retrieval and possible use at trial. A report listing time stamps and what happened at each should be provided with the link. These time stamps should match up to relevant highlights of the surveillance report as well. For instance, if in the surveillance report it states, "Mario left his residence at 2:59 and drove to the bowling alley and was seen exiting his vehicle at 3:14," those statements should match up with the video evidence provided.

- **DVD Copies:** The client should indicate clearly the number of copies needed upon completion of the case. Most firms will send one DVD unless otherwise directed. Our suggestion is to have the investigative firm burn two copies: one for you and one for defense counsel since they're going to need it anyway.

- **The Final Invoice:** Along with the summary and report findings, the investigative firm will send along an invoice. Rather than bill hourly, most firms have various package rates which you will naturally agree to during the budgeting phase of the pre-investigation.

The more thorough the final report and summary findings are, the more effectively the insurance company can determine fraud or innocence, making the investigation all the more valuable in the long run.

Following Up and Feedback

Following up with the investigative firm and offering feedback is a great way to ensure that future investigations go smoothly and that the investigative firm understands what it did, and didn't do, so well.

It is certainly within your rights to vent frustration with a case you didn't think went so well and, in fact, you may learn something while doing so. For instance, you may go back to the investigative firm and say, "You know, I'm a little frustrated, I sent you out on four different occasions and you didn't record any activity."

With open communication and thorough reporting, the investigative firm might respond by saying, "You're right, we didn't record any activity but it states very plainly on page three of the report that after recording various witness statements we learned that the mailman says he's never seen the claimant in six months, the neighbor states he never leaves his house and that, the last time he did see the claimant, he looked awful and was still in his pajamas in midday..."

Such information can be helpful in understanding that, sometimes – even often – claims are valid and investigations can't find smoke where there is no fire. What's more, the investigative firm can be helpful in nailing follow-up information that might be useful moving forward with either further investigation or legal proceedings. For instance:

- **Civil or criminal cases.** If you're going to pursue further action, either with civil or criminal proceedings, the investigative firm can assist with this.
- **How much follow-up is necessary, and when is it necessary?** Allow the investigator to do this on his/her own but if not, ask for this. For example, perhaps the claimant is an avid hunter, but hunting season doesn't start for another sixty days. To ensure that the investigation is both complete and thorough, the investigator should be back out on this subject at that time.
- **Social media.** Many claimants are sporadically active on social media, meaning that they may not reveal too much personally for one period of time, then suddenly over share with great regularly. Or, like the hunting season example from above, they may not need to be monitored until their bowling season starts back up and throughout its duration. If this is the case, the investigative firm can provide ongoing research and provide updates to ensure a thorough investigation.
- **Feedback:** Some firms offer exit interviews or feedback surveys to help rate and, potentially, improve their service. Whether it's requested of the firm or not, provide this to your agency. Not only will it help with future work for them, but it will create a stronger and better partnership for

you down the line. The investigative firm should be rated on the three following items:

o **Timeliness:** Was their investigation thorough and did they report accurate findings in a timely manner?

o **Actionable Information/Intelligence:** Did you learn anything during the investigation that you either didn't know before and/or might help put the matter to rest?

o **Communication:** How effectively did the investigative firm communicate throughout the investigation?

When you take the time to leave positive, negative or even constructive feedback, you help the investigative firm improve or refine their skill sets and also pave the way for a more collaborative work relationship in the future.

The Takeaway

All things considered, a workers' comp fraud investigation is a multi-faceted, sophisticated and (hopefully) thorough affair. By knowing what to expect at the outset, be it in terms of budgeting, specific requirements, communication and follow-up/follow-through, you can be a willing and knowledgeable participant in the investigation itself.

CHAPTER 9

How to Assess your Provider

After you've used an investigative firm to procure a successful, or even unsuccessful, investigation, it's important to provide feedback about your experience. Good, bad or ugly, if you don't provide feedback how will an investigative firm grow, learn and evolve from a poor experience?

What's more, you might need them again so giving your investigative firm specific, thoughtful feedback is the best way to ensure that they meet your needs every time you encounter a worker's comp or fraud claim in your organization.

Instead, most companies simply move on after an investigation, even if it's provided them with positive results, and particularly when it hasn't. In the case of a poor or incomplete investigation, rather than leave feedback to help improve a firm's performance, most clients will simply part ways and pledge never to use them again. But there must have been a reason why you chose that firm in the first place, and you may need them again, so helping them improve helps your chances of getting a good, or better, investigation next time. Microsoft founder, billionaire and philanthropist Bill Gates said it best when he proclaimed, "We all need people who will give us feedback. That's how we improve."

In life, work or anything that you do, if you want a positive outcome you have to measure and benchmark your progress to ensure for growth. If you want to go from Point A to Point B and what you've already been doing isn't cutting it, then you're going to have to change some things and, what's more, measure them for success along the way.

For instance, if you want to lose twenty-five pounds but your regular, daily routine of movement and eating isn't getting you anywhere, obviously you're going to have to increase the amount of physical activity you do each day (calories out) while reducing the amount or quality of food you eat (calories in). In addition, you'll have to measure your progress fairly regularly and strive to achieve certain benchmarks – losing three pounds a week, one inch around your waist, etc. – regularly if you want to achieve your goal.

Investigative firms are no different. We need to measure our growth and achieve certain benchmarks if we are to succeed in our chosen profession. One way we do that is by receiving feedback from our clients.

Providing Feedback: *Internal Controls, Systems and Key Performance Indicators (KPIs)*

Most companies *don't* necessarily have an internal system in place to rate the vendors they use and/or provide feedback – at least, not a formal one. They may have an informal board or panel that makes decisions, not only who to hire but who to – and not to – *re*-hire, but beyond that decisions are generally made on a case by case basis.

This section will cover some basic questions about *Internal Controls, Systems and Key Performance Indicators*

(KPIs) that you should be asking of yourself and your organization. Let's start with *Internal Controls and Systems.*

- **Do we have a system in the first place?** First of all, do you have a system of internal controls in place where you rate providers based on certain Key Performance Indicators, or KPIs?
- **If not, what should you look at?** If you don't have an internal system in place, consider the following questions to help create one that is personalized and targeted specifically for your organization:
- **What drives you?** To best rate a provider or vendor, you will want to assess how well they met your specific demands as an organization. Start by prioritizing what drives you as an organization.
  - o **Cost:** Is cost a major priority in your organization?
  - o **Timeliness:** Is timeliness, punctuality and attention to detail also important?
  - o **Quality:** Are you more concerned with achieving quality results?
- **Do we have enough to create a system?** Once you've considered what drives you as an organization – i.e. what's important to you – you can better create a simple system for helping rate the many providers you use on a regular basis.
- **Does the provider have a survey or account manager?** The above questions refer to what you, as an organization, can do internally to be

prepared to easily and readily provide feedback to vendors. Externally, you will want to consider whether or not the vendor has a survey or account manager. If so, be prepared to give them open, honest and constructive feedback.

- **What specific actions have been taken or could have been taken?** Another measurement you'll want to keep track of is, after you've provided feedback, what specific actions were taken and, more importantly, which steps could have been taken to act upon your feedback?
- **How do you prevent the same issue from occurring again?** Finally, consider what you or the company could have done to prevent the same issue from happening again.

Keep in mind that most investigative agencies may not have their own internal systems in place to either accept or correct feedback, so being vigilant about providing it will help you help then and, ultimately, help you in the long run if you return to use their services.

Post-Report Assessment

Once the investigative agency provides you with its final report of findings, it can be a good time to provide what we call **Post-Report Assessment** to provide the agency with feedback about their performance:

- **Format of the findings.** Consider the format of the agency's findings. Start by looking at your original request for an investigation and then compare that to the investigative agency's summary report. Then consider whether or original request ultimately addressed the original objectives. If the agency is doing its job and providing a quality report, this should be easily found in the Summary of Findings and/or Outcome section(s).

- **Did the report contain any actionable information?** Consider or not whether the report contained any information you could actually use and/or that would assist in the outcome of the investigation. A good investigative firm will use their report and, in particular, summary of findings to provide you with specific information you can use. This may come in the form of written, audio or, increasingly, video information. While sitting in on a client meeting recently I was intrigued to hear the company's CEO grumbling because the report, while containing a large amount of actionable information in written form, only contained a minute or two of video. So, increasingly, having multimedia components of a report might ultimately determine how actionable it is for the client.

- **Is it quantifiable?** Consider whether or not the summary findings are quantifiable and measurable.

- **Was the information helpful?** Finally, determine if the information was helpful or not. This can be greatly enhanced by careful planning at the outset of the investigation, and understanding by both parties of what type(s) of information the client is hoping to gain. For instance, if during our investigation we catch a suspect working when he's not supposed to, does that help or hurt the claim? The only way to know is if the parameters of the request are made, very specifically, before the investigation begins.

Ultimately, the agency's report is going to be a great guidepost for you to provide feedback because it should plainly state, in black and white, what the company did or did not do and, in many cases, how well they did it. While providing feedback, it should help you in a variety of ways.

Timeliness

Timeliness is another issue to consider in many fraud investigations:

- **Was the firm's report delivered on time and professionally?** First and foremost, the investigation should have ended on the date you wanted and a report produced shortly thereafter.
- **Were there regular updates throughout the investigation?** Throughout the investigation, there should be regular updates to inform you of what is happening and/or if any activity has been documented. We generally update the client weekly, unless otherwise specified. As a special note when providing feedback, you shouldn't dock a company for not being mind readers! In other words, if you wanted – or expected – daily updates but never specified that, how can the company know? Careful planning and open lines of communication can help the company

meet your expectations from day one of the investigation.

- **Were they regular enough to suit your needs?** Every investigation has a deadline, and it's an investigative firm's duty to meet those deadlines in a way that provides information in a timely manner so that you can examine the results before/if a case ever goes to trial.

In addition to a firm's timeliness, before or as you provide feedback, you will want to consider whether or not the time, resources and money spent provided a good return on your investment.

Investment and ROI

Everyone wants to feel like their money was well spent. In the case of a workers' comp claim investigation, consider the following:

- **What was your overall cost?** When providing feedback during a formal assessment, consider whether or not the overall cost fit not only within your budget, but the original estimate the investigative agency quoted you at the outset of the case.
- **What ratio was this to the overall investment?** In other words, consider how the investigation – and just the investigation – compared with the overall cost of the entire case.
- **Did you allocate enough resources to the claim?** When providing feedback, look within as well as without. In other words, are you allocating

enough resources for the claim to be successful? Eight hours of surveillance might sound like a lot, but is it really enough to provide results? And if you're facing a claim of $200 thousand, is spending less than a thousand dollars on surveillance enough to insulate you from liability? It's hard to determine how valuable the investment was if you didn't invest enough to begin with.

- **If you had to do this again would you?** Ultimately, consider carefully whether or not you would pursue another investigation like this and, what's more, would you do it with the same provider.

Fraud investigations require time, diligence and patience and, unfortunately, that sometimes translates into considerable cost. We had a case recently where we caught a suspect picking apples when he wasn't supposed to be doing any physical activity. It didn't happen on the first day of surveillance, or the second, or the third or even the fourth day, but on the fifth day of active surveillance.

Ultimately, video evidence of the subject in question picking apples saved the company hundreds of thousands in insurance payouts, but only because they persevered and invested enough into the investigation comparable to the claim. If they had pulled the surveillance after the first or even second eight hours, we would have never caught him on video.

Finding Your Key Performance Indicators

Key Performance Indicators, or KPIs, measure how good – or bad – an investigative agency is performing based on predetermined "indicators," or deliverables. These are different for every investigation, of course, but in general these are the KPIs that you can use to formally assess a qualified investigative agency:

- **Assign metrics to specific goals.** Before the investigation begins it is important to have not only specific goals but metrics by which to measure them. For instance...
- **On-Time Performance.** Have you set goals for timeliness? Has the vendor met those? If you've given them twenty deadlines, what is their ratio of success? Have they met half of them? Over half? If they've met eighteen of their internal deadlines but missed two, is it really fair to ding them for on-time performance when, after all, they have an eighty percent success ratio?
- **Timely Communication.** What are your expectations around "timely" communication? Every day? Every hour? After every six- to eight-hour block of surveillance? Whatever metrics you've established to measure performance, was that expectation met?
- **Actionable Information/Intelligence.** How do you quantify information or intelligence as actionable? In other words, how do you define results? Written and verbal reports help an investigative agency log their time and also their

results, and can be a good way to put metrics around your expectations.

- **Were the Case Objectives Met?** Having firm objectives for the case helps the investigative agency achieve better results. The more specific those objectives are at the outset, the more clearly they are stated, the simply they are to achieve. For instance, you may have five objectives you want the investigator to meet, such as "Does the claimant live at the residence?" and/or "Does the claimant own the residence?" These types of clearly defined objectives not only help determine the scope of the investigation but also lets the investigative agency provide simple "yes" or "no" answers.

- **Quality of the Field Investigator?** Rating a field investigator's performance should be as simple as rating a fine meal after you've had dessert. For instance, a field investigator with little to no experience might sit in his vehicle and note, every hour on the hour, that there has been "no claimant activity." A seasoned investigator, meanwhile, will typically conduct a more proactive investigation and provide more specific notes such as, "While speaking to a neighbor under a pretext I verified that the claimant is always home," or "I observed the mailman walking by, approached and was able to determine that the claimant lived at the address specified." While the result in both cases is the same "no claimant activity," the differences in the quality of the field investigator vary wildly.

- **Quality of the Video?** Video is becoming increasingly important to fraud investigations, so when providing feedback to an agency this will be a topic of discussion you will want to address. You will want to rate not just the amount of video – one hour, five hours or fifty hours – but also the quality of that video. Was the video choppy or of high quality so that the claimant's fraudulent activity was easily observable to the uninitiated? In the heat of surveillance, it can be tempting for inexperienced investigators to get any video at the expense of quality, running around and operating a "shaky cam." But will that evidence hold up in court if it's impossible to determine what, actually, is happening?
- **Cost/ROI?** One way to measure and evaluate the cost of the investigation and your return on investment is to compare the money spent on the field investigation to the overall investigation, and comparing them accurately.
- **Helpful to overall claim?** Consider whether or not the investigation was useful to the overall claim. You can do so, easily and effectively, by simply looking at the previous bullet points listed above this one and assigning a number, on a scale of 1 to 10, to each one. Tallying the numbers should help you get, and give, an overall picture of the firm's performance while encouraging you to make special note of facets of the investigation that earned a particularly high, or low, rating.
- **Establish baselines for acceptable goals for each category.** Once you rate each facet of the

organization, from video quality to timeliness to communication, establish a baseline for acceptable goals. Hitting a "ten" in each category may be ideal, but not entirely realistic, so perhaps "eight" is your baseline for whether or not a category of the investigation is acceptable.

- **Measure.** Once you have "graded" the agency in each category, you can assign an overall grade of "A," "B," "C" and down the line. This lets them know, quickly and accurately, how they've performed.

- **Determine your "A" players.** With a grade firmly in place, you can best know how to rank an investigative agency and, if they fall out of your "A" player ranking, whether or not to use them again. This kind of feedback is also helpful to let the agency know when they might have to tighten up and get back to basics.

- **Hold others accountable by sharing!** Finally, sharing the feedback lets the investigative agency know where they might be slipping or where they've done exceedingly well.

As with your own company, most investigative agencies in this industry hold themselves to a high standard. By assessing yours on these key performance indicators, you can help the organization continue to keep its level of quality high or, if it fell below expectations, help it get better for the next investigation – or even *your* next investigation.

The Takeaway

Investigating for fraud is never fun, but in today's modern and sophisticated climate, it is often quite necessary. When and if you find yourself in a position to defend yourself against such claims, it's important to hire a qualified and professional investigative firm. Providing this type of feedback helps companies like mine attain, and maintain, the highest professional standards in the investigative industry.

CHAPTER 10

Case Studies in Fraud

Rather than summarize our earlier chapters or spend any more time on the background of fraud, I'd like to spend a little time in our last chapter together exposing the decisions of two actual fraud cases. Doing so will bring together everything we've talked about so far in this book – from what type of investigation to run, to paying attention to details and investing in a thorough investigation, and how attention to these details can result in positive findings for you and your workers' comp fraud claim.

In this chapter we'll highlight summary briefs of two actual fraud cases and I'll quote from actual findings so you can see how the work we do – surveillance, video recording and even social media investigation – can result in saving companies hundreds of thousands of claims in one-time or ongoing settlement payments for fraudulent claims:

Case Study # 1: *"Clear evidence of significant symptom magnification..."*

Our first case involves a man we'll call "Jerry" (not his real name). Jerry was a machinist for a large, self-insured employer. He worked there for five or more years without

Mario S. Pecoraro

incident until one day he suffered an injury while working as a machinist. He was eventually classified as PPD, or "Permanent Partial Disability" due to issues resulting from his accident that were affecting his lower back.

A note here on lower back injuries: they're very common in fraud cases. They are hard to prove and/ or disprove, and affect almost every type of work employees do – physical labor, sitting and standing – and thus very easy to file a claim for.

At the time of the original accident Human Resources was made aware of the situation and, after some initial paperwork and, since they were self-insured, turned the matter over to the third party administrator, or TPA. The TPA immediately opened up a file on it as well as assigning it to an adjuster.

Over the course of several IMEs, or Independent Medical Exams, the adjuster learned that Jerry was not only not returning to work but had no interest or desire in doing so. Ultimately, because of his permanent partial disability, Jerry expressed a desire to settle a claim and effectively retire.

After learning of this decision, the company, the HR department and the independent adjuster realized the stakes were suddenly much higher than originally imagined. A PPD finding for a man of Jerry's age, neither young nor old, would mean a considerable settlement figure for both the insurance company and the company Jerry had worked for. Neither expressed a desire to support Jerry for the rest of his life, particularly if fraud were involved.

Digging deeper into the case, Jerry's employer and the insurance adjuster they'd hired noticed several "red flags" that were present during his series of independent medical exams. That's when we got involved.

Over the course of several days of eyewitness, audio and video surveillance, we witnessed Jerry doing all kinds of things he purportedly told his doctors he could no longer do: kneeling, squatting, using a hammer and drill and doing home repairs that were well within the scope of the work he told his employer – and various medical examiners – he could no longer do.

What's important to note about this case was the early involvement and cooperation of the employer, HR and the outside auditor. Everyone agreed there was something going on and were all committed to doing something about it. As a result, they committed to a thorough and reasonable investigation, during which we were able to attain quality evidence to prove fraud.

As a result of that investigation, the court found the following: "Based upon a review of the record, a finding is made that claimant has violated WCL section 114-a in his assertions to practitioners, with respect to his physical incapacity as it relates to the instant claim. Furthermore, it is held that claimant's physical activities, as reflected in the DVD, comport with the opinion of Dr. Kirkpatrick, of no more than a mild residual disability, if any, with many non-organic and non-anatomic signs findings and clear evidence of significant symptom magnification on serial exams including far exaggerated response to light touch."

In addition, the findings expressed that "The video from 11/1/11... contrasts to the report of Dr. Kirkpatrick where the claimant indicated he oversaw his son performing the work, did not work himself and maybe hammered down an exposed nail or two."

As a result of these findings Jerry's benefits were cut off and further payments were suspended, resulting in an immediate savings to the insurance carrier and Jerry's employer. While no criminal case was brought, all parties agreed that it was certainly a "viable option" in the future, should they choose to do so.

Case Study # 2: *Case Closed!*

Our second case involves a man we'll call "Phil" (not his real name). Phil was working in maintenance for a large employer when he suffered an injury that was later classified as temporarily totally disabled. This type of finding generally indicates that the employee is, for a certain amount of time, totally disabled but that this isn't necessarily a permanent condition such as when someone becomes paralyzed.

As in our earlier case, Human Resources immediately got involved. Since this was a large employer they actually had a workers' comp department, which the case was ultimately handed to. Also self-insured, the company sought the assistance of an independent adjuster who went about insuring that Phil underwent several independent medical exams. During those exams HR and the insurance adjuster noted the presence of several "red flags" and decided to open a fraud investigation.

Phil's case is unique because it was a case where social media played a significant role in proving there actually was fraud. Not only did video surveillance prove that Phil was more active than his diagnosis would indicate, or allow for, but he was actively running a successful snow plow business – and actively soliciting clients online using social media.

In this case, though social media surveillance – which as we know is becoming increasingly important – we were able to catch Phil in various instances seeking and finding clients for his business online.

Clued into his side business activity through his social media surveillance we were able to use that information to strategically record him actually running a snow plow at not just one but various job sites. In addition, we were able to ascertain through recorded evidence that he obtained funds (i.e. got paid) for doing such work, which is a big element of proving workers' comp fraud and one that can often be hard to prove. As you can imagine, employers, insurance companies and various legal agencies frown on employees being paid for doing outside work while on a disability claim – and receiving benefits – from their previous job.

During a hearing Phil gave testimony that basically denied all wrongdoing that we found during the investigation: he hadn't operated a snowplow, couldn't operate a snowplow, hadn't actively advertised for work on social media, nor had he received compensation for that type of work since he'd been on disability.

Ultimately, the judge weighed our evidence against Phil's testimony and made the following judgment: "I find the claimant's testimony regarding his work status, his work ability and his operation of a snowplow business in 2104 incredible. I find that the claimant, when confronted with evidence that he was seeking snow plow business by his Facebook posts, denied seeking customers and business with explanations that were not believable and were not credible."

Furthermore, the judge expressed, "I find claimant knowingly made false statements or representations as to material facts for the purpose of influencing a determination regarding his compensation benefits and that the mandatory and discretionary penalties are applicable. Claimant is disqualified from receiving future indemnity benefits in this case..."

What's important to note about Phil's case was that a mere surface investigation would not have dug deep enough to discover the true extent of Phil's fraud. Phil wasn't necessarily working around his home, so the usual surveillance wouldn't have caught his elaborate ruse.

Instead, we were clued into his activities – and even the location of those activities – through active and routine social media surveillance, which is something many companies still don't include in their "basic" investigation. Had we not covered a variety of facets in our investigation, not only would Phil's employer been unsuccessful in disputing his claim but in all likelihood Phil would still be in the system today, collecting those benefits to which he was not entitled.

The Takeaway

I think both of the above cases make a good point about having thorough, timely and detail-oriented investigations as part of the workers' comp fraud process. While not every case we take on results in such findings, many do and that's because we pride ourselves in being thorough and diligent in investigating insurance fraud.

One topic that I wanted to address before I leave is that of criminal prosecution. Now, despite finding fraud in both of the above cases, both "Jerry" and "Phil" were never criminally prosecuted, although that option certainly exists.

I find that many clients avoid criminal prosecution because they don't want to be perceived as bullies throwing people in jail for fraud. However, many I speak to consider the threat of criminal prosecution as a bargaining chip, or leverage, against future fraud or settling current fraud cases.

At any rate, I hope you enjoyed these case studies as a conclusion of how successful workers' comp fraud cases are resolved. If you or someone you know is in the midst of such a case, or simply wants to avoid one, I encourage you to speak to a qualified fraud investigator and educate yourself about the presence of fraud – and how to avoid it.

While doing so, please visit my site at www. allianceinvestigative.com to discover a wealth of free resources on this topic. As always, I'd love to hear about your case and how it was, or perhaps could be, resolved successfully. I hope you've found this book useful and think you'll find the many resources available at my site a worthwhile addition to the quality content found here.

Printed in the United States
By Bookmasters